P9-AZW-673

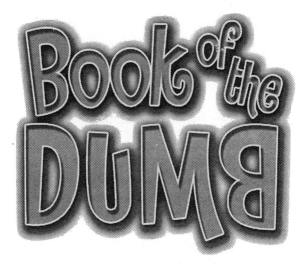

Uncle John's PRESENTS

Book of the DUMB

John Scalzi

Portable Press
San Diego, CA, and Ashland, OR

This book is dedicated to Deven Desai, who has long suspected
stupidity is everywhere. Here is your proof, Devin.

UNCLE JOHN'S PRESENTS
BOOK OF THE DUMB

Copyright © 2003 by Portable Press.
All rights reserved. No part of this book may be used or
reproduced in any manner whatsoever without written
permission, except in the case of brief quotations
embodied in critical articles or reviews.

"*Uncle John's Presents*" is a trademark of Portable Press.

For information, write
Portable Press
5880 Oberlin Drive, San Diego, CA 92121
e-mail: *unclejohn@advmkt.com*

Project Team:
Allen Orso, Publisher
JoAnn Padgett, Director, Editorial and Production
Jennifer Thornton, Project Editor
Stephanie Spadaccini, Editor
Amy Shapiro, Composition
Cover design by Michael Brunsfeld (brunsfeldo@comcast.net)

ISBN: 1-59223-149-7

Library of Congress Catalog-in-Publication Data (applied for)

Printed in the United States of America
First printing: October 2003

03 04 05 06 07 10 9 8 7 6 5 4 3 2 1

CONTENTS

BEAUTY BONERS
A Bad Era for Sensible Shoes 3
One More Item for the "Do Not
Place in Microwave" List 32
Next Time, He Should Go for a
Little Sequined Number 63
Not the Record to Hold If You
Want to Meet Groovy Chicks
83
He's Not Exactly Happy About
Those "Skorts," Either 154

CAREER STOPPERS
Give Him a Pink Slip 123
No Good Deed Goes Unpunished
178
Turn on Your Art Light 179
A Hard Knock Life 219
Dumb, For Goodness' Sake 291

COFFEE, TEA, OR ?
Roll Call 11
She Screamed for Ice Cream 181
You Found *What* in My Freezer? 239
When Life Hands you Lemons,
Make Sure Your Permits Are in
Order 255

CRAZY CRITTERS
Sometimes the Insect Wins 129
Mama Bears Down on the Crowd
168
A Dog Day Afternoon 176
So Much for Puppy Love 234
Like a Rat in a Daze 280
For Gerbil's Sake! 303

CRIME DOESN'T PAY
Arms and the Man 9
Take a Bite Out of Crime 114

Confidential Communication
Gone Wrong 145
If He'd Taken the Ice Cream, He'd
Probably Be Looking at a Felony
160
From Doo-Doo to Deep Doo-Doo
253
A Taxing Situation 257

DAZED AND CONFUSED
Harry Potter and the Reality-
Impaired Fan 22
Up in Smoke 35
Not Very Cool 79
Bang! You're Dumb 111
Welcome to Freedom, You're
Under Arrest 259
Beekeep, I'll Have a Stinger 262

DEARLY BELOVED
Court Order: Deceased Spouse
Must Pay Alimony 21
Don't Drive Angry. Don't Crash
Angry Either. 72
Ultimate Mellow Harsher 82
Dear Diary: I Hope My Wife
Doesn't Read You! 211
Dial "D" For Divorce 271

**DRIVING WITH YOUR
LIGHTS OUT**
Slow Rider 1
A Combustible Situation 17
Bad Parents, in Cars 108
Dagnabbit! The Gas Pedal Moved
On Its Own! 208
When Gas Supplies Come to a
Dead Stop 267
Note to Self: 911 Doesn't Take
Requests 273

DUMB MOVIE FESTIVAL

From Justin to Kelly 7
Kangaroo Jack 37
The League of Extraordinary Gentlemen 77
The Adventures of Pluto Nash 149
Swept Away 173
Ballistic: Ecks vs. Sever 193
Glitter 209
Freddy Got Fingered 236
3000 Miles to Graceland 251
Battlefield Earth 278
Dungeons & Dragons 299

EXECRABLE EDUCATION

Another Third Will Have to Sit at the Nerd Table at Lunch 55
Golden Rule Days 180
What the Hack? 213
As Far As You Know, This Article Is 100% Original 216
Thank God It Wasn't a Medical Exam 226
Psyched Out 301

GOVERNMENT GOOFUPS

Yipes! Stripes! 31
The High Cost of Sitting 43
Wait Till You Hear What They Call Their Hard Liquor! 102
Paging Senator Ryder 126
If You're Seeing Double, Does That Mean You've Voted Twice? 137
A Snafu at Headquarters 151
Taking a Yen for Pachinko a Little Too Far 185
Your Cat Is in for a Shock 198
Dumb Municipal Codes in Action 214
He'll Need One Heck of a Wireless Connection 231

HISTORICAL DUMBOSITY

The Zimmermann Telegram 12
Bad Food Ideas 89
Louis XVI's Money Problems 182
Donkey Kong Kraziness 221
When Will They Ever Learn? 243
Not So Golden Oldie 274
Another Megalomaniac Has a Go At It 308

HOLD YOUR PEACE

Chicken Legs! Chicken Legs! 50
The 411 on 911 92
Later in the Day, the NRA Went Through the Halls Shooting Blanks 147
Dear God: Next Time Send an Mail 282

HOW BEASTLY

Not What Is Usually Meant by "Mixed Media" 33
You Can Buy Bullets in the Gift Shop 70
For God's Sake Don't Go After a Grizzly with Endust 139
Om, Om, Ow! 143
A Fishy Premise 170
See You Later Alligator 197

LEGAL EAGLES, NOT

And Iowa's Streets Will Flow Cornhusker Red! 23
On the Other Hand, Would You Want This Guy on Your Jury? 98
Jailhouse Lawyer 113
Mon Dieu! Stop the Music! 132
Bloody Dumb 157
How to Annoy a Judge, Tip #4655 228
Born to Be Bad 247

MISCELLANEOUS, BUT STILL DUMB

Dude, Where's My Condo? 5
First We Take Austria, Then Liechtenstein Will Fall Like a Plump Grape 87
Dubious Décor Award 94
The Toilet Paper–Dispensing PDA Costs Extra 134
Hakenkreuzing for a Bruising 141
Grandfather Cluck 156
Jewelry to Spare, Apparently 163
Balloonatic 165
This Rescue Was All Wet 175
A Gun in the Oven 204
How Not to Hail a Taxi 227
Happy Birthday, Dumb-Ass 230
That's One Lucky Man 306

MONEY MAYHEM

A Powerful Clerical Error 19
Money for Nothing 41
That's Some Bank Error 75
You Can Put Them Right Next to Your Fake Credit Cards 85
Hands Down, the Stickiest Tax Situation Yet 104
Dumpl8s 152

ONE TOO MANY FOR THE ROAD

Baby, You Can Drive My Car—in Seven Years 25
A Stupid Excuse That Wasn't 44
How Not to Cleanse Your Palate 52
Honesty Is the Best Policy, Except in Circumstances Like These 96
Driven to Drink 106
DUI Double Trouble 289
Another One for the "Expecting Too Much From Fermented Potatoes" File 295

PERFORMING ARTS?

A Capitol Performance 58
I'd Kill for This Part! 97
Cops! Live on MTV! 122
The Russian Version of Sing-Sing 232

PLEASE DON'T TELL ME THAT...

A Cheesy Airport Security Story 48
Canada, My Canada 57
Stupid Air Traffic Controller Tricks 130
Is That a Bomb in Your Shoe, or Are You Just Happy to See Me? 189
Bono's Hat Trick 206
What's More, Miming a Bomb Threat Isn't Cool, Either 264

THE REALLY STUPID QUIZ

Escaped Prisoners 29
Wacky World Leaders 39
Artsy-Fartsy 68
Sensitivity 191
Those Crazy Teens! 202
Those Disturbing Animals! 224
Bureaucracy in Action 249
The World of Fashion 269
Stupidity at Work 284
The Rocky Road to Love 297

SEXCAPADES

And Here I Thought Gutvik Was a Kind of Fish 26
The Hurtingest Man in the World 46
She Popped the Clutch. He Put It in Gear. Heh Heh Heh. 187
Double Your Pleasure 220
You Oughta Be in Pictures. Or Not. 241

SPORTS NUTS

#1 at Wimbledon 65
He Gets First Place in Something,
   All Right 74
Just Say No, Except to Us 100
50,000 Volts Is Just God's Way of
   Telling You to Play Through 127
The Running of the Morons 199

THAT'S ENTERTAINMENT!

Train Wreck TV 60
Give 'Em 15 Minutes and You'll
   Have the Screenplay for *Gigli*
   115
Pay for TV? That's Communism!
   117
The U.S. Flag: Love It or Move to
   Norway! 120
Fan Service 158

TIPS FOR STUPID
   CRIMINALS

You Look Awfully Familiar 28
Tool Time 36
"Hi, I'm Here to Fix Your..." 66
A Bad Disguise 73
That Divan Looks Divine 119
Because I Look Good in Pumps
   125
Smile You're on Candid Stadium
   Cam 162
Restrain Yourself 167
As Dumb As Watching Paint Dry
   177
No License to Drive 184
I've Positively ID'd Myself 188

TRAVEL TRAVAILS

Anatomy of a Dumb Excuse: The
   Nekkid Pilots 53
That's What You Get for Cutting
   in Line 80

It Was Just Like the Love Boat,
   Except for Those Darn Federal
   Agents 195
Now For the In-Flight
   Entertainment 286

WHAT! YOU'VE GOT
MORE TIPS FOR STUPID
CRIMINALS?

It Takes a Thief 201
He'll Be Calling from a Cell, Not
   on One 218
Speling Maters 223
Dubya Dollars 229
Throw the Book At Me, Why
   Don't You? 238
The Getaway 248
Tax Dodge 261
What a Flop! 266
Jail Break 281
Armed and Not Dangerous 288
Excuse Me, but Do You Know
   Where I Can Buy a Gun? 293
Don't Get Caught with Your Hand
   in the Till 305

The Answer Zone 311
The Last Page 312

ACKNOWLEDGMENTS

I had a big old ball of fun writing this book, and much of the reason for that is that I had help and encouragement from some great folks. Here are some of them.

First, the "Beta Testers" who read the pieces as I cranked them out and offered suggestions and comments. They are (in no particular order): Daniel Mainz, Kathy Haggerty, Nicolas Condon, Bill Dickson, Heather Coon, Roger Baker, Mykal Burns, Stephanie Lynn, Sue Irvin, Jeffrey Brown, Natasha Kordus, Ed Thibodeau, Lisa Ferris, and Cian Chang. I'm sure I missed a couple; you know who you are and I thank you.

Among the beta testers, I'd like to single out Bill Peschel, who offered editing suggestions for just about every entry. Thanks, Bill, I really appreciated it. I've said it before, but it's worth saying one more time: you rock.

The writing of this book would not have been possible without the existence of the Internet and the World Wide Web (well, it would have been possible, it just would have driven me insane), so thanks to Tim Berners-Lee for inventing the Web and those crazy kids at ARPANET for thinking up this whole "Net" thing.

But more immediately, mad crazy props to Drew Curtis and all the members of Fark.com. If you don't know Fark, it's a site whose members link to strange and bizarre news stories from all around the world, thus making my job that much easier. For doing so, Fark.com gets my vote for the Greatest Web Site Ever. Thanks, Drew; thanks, Farksters.

At Portable Press, I'd like to thank the people who actually put the book together and put the text into workable order: Allen Orso, JoAnn Padgett, Jennifer Thornton, Amy Shapiro, and Amanda Wilson. Michael Brunsfeld put together the cover: I thank him.

Thanks to Kristine and Athena Scalzi for being my wife and child, respectively. They're harder jobs than one might think.

PREFACE

What is stupidity?

What separates man from the rest of the animal kingdom? Contrary to popular belief, it is not our ability to use tools, or carry on conversation, or make fruity tropical drinks, since animals have been observed doing all of these things. (There is nothing more amusing than watching a crow make a mai tai.) No, what separates humanity from the beasts of the field, the air, and the sea is one small, simple concept:

Stupidity.

Consider a person who, say, uses her cigarette lighter to peer into a gas tank to see if it's full. Do you hold her stupidity against her? Sure you do. She ought to know *better*. She's being *stupid*.

But what is stupidity? Well, it's not just being unintelligent, since so-called "smart" people do stupid things all the time (just watch an engineering student try to get a date). Stupidity is *the unwillingness to appreciate the consequences of your actions*. From the thief who leaves a credit application at the store he's just robbed, to the deposed king who gives himself away by asking for directions out of the country, stupidity happens when people have the ability to think things through but *choose not to*.

In other words, stupidity is punishment for not thinking. Hey, you don't even have to think well. You just have to think. You can't blame animals for not thinking things through—they're not designed for it—but you can blame humans. The capacity for stupidity is unique to our species. No one else has it. It is our birthright, the very essence of humanity.

Which brings us to why we're all here today. In your hands is *Book of the Dumb*—a celebration of stupidity. In its pages you'll find example after example of people doing remarkably stupid things—most of these within just the last year alone. These people come from all walks of life: some are rich, some are poor. Some are college graduates, some probably didn't get through grade school. Some are criminals, some are upstanding citizens. Some are Americans, others come from all around the world. Some are young, some are old. Some are women, some are men. The only thing they all have in common is that if you went up to them afterward and asked them why they acted so stupidly, they'd probably just shrug and say, "I guess I wasn't thinking at the time."

In addition to these tales of modern imbecility, we've put in some recurring features to make your reading experience more fun.

- **Tips for Stupid Criminals** provide critical insight to those who need it most—criminals who are three lockpicks short of a full set.
- **The Dumb Movie Festival** highlights some of the most inexplicable films of the last few years.
- **The Really Stupid Quiz** challenges you to spot the real stupid story among made-up ringers. It's tougher than you think.
- **Historical Dumbosity** provides tales of stupidity from days gone by, to assure you that humanity isn't getting stupider, it's merely maintaining its status quo.

We hope the stories you find in *Book of the Dumb* will make you laugh and make you think. Remember: the more you think, the less chance you have of something similar happening to you. Stupidity may separate us from the animals, but it's avoiding stupidity that can separate you from the crowd.

Enjoy!

—John Scalzi

FOREWORD

Welcome to Uncle John's Presents latest (and strangest) production . . . *Book of the Dumb*.

What is it, you ask? We like to think of this book as a wild and wacky road trip through all the bizarre, harebrained, hair-raising, and just plain dumb things that people do, spiced with a healthy dash of fascinating facts on dumb movies, dumb crooks, dumb deeds through history, and so much more. For example:

- The thief who robbed a woman and then took a nap on her sofa instead of leaving with his loot.
- The man who refuted his tax bill because he disputed the amount of his illegal drug proceeds.
- A woman who tried to pass a stolen ID to the person she lifted it from.
- The man who set his house on fire trying to eradicate mosquitoes.
- A sister who filed criminal charges against her brother for stealing food from her home.
- A manager who had an employee strip-searched because of a call he got from a "policeman" telling him to do so.
- Women who have foot surgery just to fit into designer shoes.
- The spreadsheet error that cost a company $24 million.

Some of it will amaze you, some of it may horrify you a little, some of it is just plain weird, but most of all, we hope it will entertain and amuse you; because as we all know, the human mind can be a strange place to visit.

So bring your seats to their full upright positions (forget those tray tables) and fasten your seatbelts because this is going to be a bumpy ride . . .

Go with the flow!

—Uncle Al

SLOW RIDER

The star of this story, "Sid," decided that the time had come to get a lawn tractor. No more slaving behind a lawn mower for him—from now on, he was going to ride, whirling blades under his feet, and shave his lawn into submission. With his mind on his mowing and his mowing on his mind, Sid headed to the neighborhood Lowe's in Connecticut Commons, Connecticut, slapped down his $1,400, and got a snazzy new Troy-Bilt tractor ready to ride.

Now all he had to do was to get it home. Lowe's offered home delivery for $55, but apparently that was too rich for Sid's blood; he refused. The tractor was *ready to ride*, darn it, and that's what he was going to do. Sid straddled his new machine, fired it up, opened up the throttle—and raced home at the tractor's top speed of 10 to 12 miles per hour on city streets. His wife followed behind him in the family minivan, hazard lights flashing, to make sure he wasn't flattened by a passing car.

Low-Speed Chase
Shortly thereafter the cops were tipped off and raced to the scene. Sid, perhaps realizing a high-speed chase was not in the cards, pulled over and was issued a ticket for driving an unlicensed motor vehicle.

It seems that Connecticut, in its stately wisdom, considers a lawn tractor to be a motor vehicle if you're not actually mowing grass at the time of operation. If only Sid had known, he could have given the road shoulder a nice trim and avoided the ticket entirely.

"It had headlights. I guess they thought they could drive it," arresting officer David Posadas said. "He had the lights on."

The ticket, incidentally, cost $78—more than the cost of delivery. To add insult to injury, Sid was told that he could not drive the rest of the way home; he'd have to find another way to get the tractor to his house or it would be towed (to an impound lot, not his house). Sid ended up renting a van.

The moral: Cough it up for delivery, or you'll be the one getting the trim.

Source: *Hartford Courant*

* * *

NOT QUITE A HOME IMPROVEMENT

If you live in Ebensburg, Pennsylvania, hold off on inflating that kiddie pool. A couple who had blown up an inflatable pool in their yard was told by the local government that they'd need a building permit for the pool or they might get fined. Ebensburg's zoning laws require pools deeper than 18 inches to be fenced. Zoning officials say they're just doing their job, but as the husband of this couple put it: "Who would think that you would need government permission to buy a $49 inflatable at Wal-Mart and put it in your driveway?" In other news, there's a sale on fencing at Wal-Mart!

Source: Associated Press

A BAD ERA FOR SENSIBLE SHOES

In *Cinderella* (and we're talking about the *real* fairy tale, not the sanitized, Disney version), Cinderella loses her slipper and the prince's men search the kingdom looking for the tiny foot that fit it, with the payoff that whoever's foot fit would marry the prince and one day become queen.

Cinderella's evil stepsisters were so determined to succeed that when it came time to try the slipper on, they chopped off their own toes to get their feet to fit.

Well, it didn't work, of course, and in the end Cinderella married the prince while the evil stepsisters had their eyes pecked out by birds—without their toes, they couldn't run away. We can't understand why Disney didn't want to animate this version of the story. The real moral to the Cinderella story: Despite what you may think, some shoes just aren't worth the pain.

This Little Piggy Went to the Doctor

Apparently some women would beg to differ: the *Sunday Times* of Australia reported in August 2003 on the latest trend for some women who are clearly far too concerned about fashion: reconstructive foot surgery to fit those toes into the latest Jimmy Choos and other high-end shoes. The story profiles two women who had their feet done for their shoes' sake; one of them is described as a "fashion victim of the cult for Manolo Blahnik," whose foot surgery included shortening one toe, repositioning another, and cutting off a bunion, and who scheduled the surgery in February in order to be ready for the summer shoe-wearing season.

Ironically, the sanest people in this story turn out to be the foot doctors themselves. Dr. Suzanne Levine, who does hundreds of foot surgeries every year, said: "I've had people ask for toe liposuction. I tell them to go see a therapist." The cost of one of these operations: about $5,000 or so. We were praying this was one of those hoaxes you hear so much about until we found supporting interviews from a third source with both the fashion victim and Dr. Levine. It's true. Horribly, painfully true.

Just Take 'Em Off, Lady

Our first reaction when shoes make our feet feel bad is to stop wearing them. So for everyone who'd cut up their own feet for the sake of fashion, we have two pieces of advice. First, get a grip. Second, watch for flocks of vengeful, pecking birds. Or at least learn how to sprint to safety in your Manolo Blahniks. Mind your toes.

Sources: *Sunday Times* (Australia), WHDH-TV

* * *

"There are well-dressed foolish ideas just as there are well-dressed fools."

—**Nicolas Chamfort**

DUDE,
WHERE'S MY CONDO?

A nd now, the *Book of the Dumb* Players present *Dude, Where's My Condo?* A play in four acts!

ACT I: *A Condo in Summit County, Colorado.*
The Occupants, BRENDA and JEFF, stand by the door.

Brenda: What a gorgeous night! We should do something with this glorious evening. Something together.
Jeff: I suggest drinking until we can barely think.
Brenda: Yeah, that works for me. (*They exit.*)

ACT II: *A Condo in Summit County, later that same night.*
BRENDA and JEFF enter through the door and woozily turn on the lights.

Brenda: Oh my God, we've been robbed!
Jeff: They took everything! They took our TV! They took our paintings! They took our kitchen appliances!
Brenda (*in her underwear*): They took my clothes!
Jeff: Weren't you wearing clothes when we left?
Brenda: I don't remember. It was so many drinks ago.

ACT III: *The same condo later that night.*
BRENDA and JEFF are standing around with a POLICEMAN.

Policeman: Perhaps your landlord can shed some light on this robbery.
Jeff: I hope so! I miss my stuff!
Brenda: And I miss my clothes!

(enter LANDLORD)

Landlord: I have good news. I found all of Brenda and Jeff's material possessions!
Policeman: And where might they be?
Landlord: In their condo, two buildings over. These drunken fools are in a vacant condo I'm trying to sell.

ACT IV: The Summit County Sheriff's Office

Policeman: We had to take Brenda and Jeff into protective custody. She had a blood alcohol count of .193 and he had one of .238.
Landlord: And we never did find out what happened to Brenda's clothes.
Policeman: Hey, what are you doing here?
Landlord: I was led to understand there would be doughnuts.

THE END

Source: TheDenverChannel.com

DUMB MOVIE FESTIVAL: FROM JUSTIN TO KELLY (2003)

Welcome to the Dumb Movie Festival, in which we, uh, celebrate massive expenditures of movie cash in the pursuit of exceptionally questionable cinematic ideas—and taste. As you might imagine, quite a few films fit this particular profile, so for the sake of mercy, we're confining ourselves to the last few years. Can you take the pain? Sure you can!

Our Entry: *From Justin to Kelly*, starring Kelly Clarkson and Justin Guarini

The Plot (Such As It Is): *American Idol* finalists Kelly Clarkson and Justin Guarini play fictionalized versions of themselves as spring break partiers who meet in a girl's bathroom and decide to fall for each other despite having the romantic chemistry of damp socks and an armadillo. This leads to spontaneous, poorly choreographed dance numbers on the beach done to songs that you won't remember even as you listen to them. At least it was an excuse for everyone in the film to get some sun.

Fun Fact: The film was originally slated as a direct-to-video release, but then theater owners complained that they wanted part of the *American Idol* action, thereby proving that, per screenwriter William Goldman's famous dictum regarding Hollywood, "theater owners don't know anything either."

Total North American Box Office: $4,922,166
(source: The-Numbers.com). Guess they should have
gone the straight-to-video route.

The Critics Rave!

"How bad is *From Justin to Kelly*? Set in Miami during spring
break, it's like *Grease: The Next Generation* acted out by the
food-court staff at SeaWorld."—*Entertainment Weekly*

"*From Justin to Kelly* is the movie equivalent of general anes-
thetic; the handful of unwary civilians emerging from yesterday's first show at the Union Square looked like they had
just awoken from a very deep sleep."—*New York Post*

"Some people wait a lifetime for a turkey like this—and for
them, *From Justin to Kelly* will provide a holiday feast. Not
since Diana Ross and Brandy's *Double Platinum* has there
been such a spectacularly wretched musical melodrama . . .
The screenplay, by Kim Fuller, is the perfect plot for those
who find *Grease* overly complicated and obtuse."
—*Kalamazoo Gazette*

"It would be easier to care about the fate of Justin and Kelly's
relationship if they had an ounce of chemistry between them.
These kids are not so much Frankie and Annette as Donny
and Marie. Their big kissing scene holds a lurid fascination:
You almost feel you're watching something unseemly."
—*Orlando Sentinel*

"Justin meets Kelly. Justin loses Kelly. Dialogue coach
checks into hospital with self-inflicted head wound."
—*Efilmcritic.com*

ARMS AND THE MAN

The Scene: State Correctional Institution at Pine Grove in Pennsylvania. Two prisoners are standing around observing the stainless-steel toilet that comes—no extra charge!—as just one of the many amenities of that fine establishment. Finally, our first prisoner, "Jed," speaks.

Jed: I knew a guy that got his arm stuck in one of them toilets.
Jud (*the other prisoner*): Ah, you're nuts. That's just one of them prison legends, like the one about the guy that escaped with a spoon and a bar of soap. You can't stick your arm that far into a toilet.
Jed: I'll bet you could if you tried.
Jud: You're wrong, and I'll prove it to you by sticking my arm into this toilet.

And so it came to pass that Jud did stick his arm into the toilet, just to show that it could not, in fact, get stuck. Whereupon Jud discovered that his pal's tale rang true; his arm had become lodged in the stainless-steel can.

The Arms Race

This is because Jed wasn't lying: firefighters had been called to the same prison to "free" another inmate whose arm had become trapped in the john. The previous inmate's excuse for sticking his arm into the toilet was that he had dropped a bar of soap into it and was trying to retrieve it. Apparently Jud, now up to his forearm in the prison loo, hadn't been in jail at the time of the first incident.

So the firefighters were called out once again to remove a toilet from a prisoner's arm; to do so they had to unbolt the thing from the floor and use an air chisel to cut the thing off. Jud, in addition to his original crime of aggravated assault, now faced more sanctions, and owed the Commonwealth of Pennsylvania the cost of a new stainless-steel toilet. That's a lot of hours stamping license plates.

Source: *Pittsburgh Post-Gazette*

* * *

CHUTZPAH, INDIAN STYLE

A man accused of forgery and cheating the Indian army decided that this whole court thing was a real waste of his time. So he tried to bribe his judge by passing her a note with his bail application: "You should release me immediately and also decide the case in my favour. Once I am released, I shall furnish your fee for this favour by cheque."

Now, aside from the legal ramifications involved, why might the judge not want to do this? That's right: that forgery charge. The enraged judge had the defendant read the note aloud in court, and then tossed him into jail. Bail was denied, of course.

Source: Ananova

ROLL CALL

There are some things the public doesn't need to know about its government—things our elected officials do that are so heinous, so disturbing, so horrifying, that they're best kept from the population at large. For example, eating cinnamon rolls.

Yes, "cinnamon rolls" was the excuse given by the Denver City Council for banning the cameras of a public television station from a session of the council. Council-woman Jeanne Faatz made the request days in advance. Apparently she thought that the televised image of elected representatives chowing down on sticky buns would be too much for the populace to handle.

Now, coincidentally, the cinnamon rolls were consumed at a council meeting that touched on the issue of the extremely cash-strapped Denver government possibly having to lay off city workers. Which you might think would be a good reason not to televise the proceedings; after all, everyone loves a surprise, especially when it involves your job. But no, the council insisted it was the cinnamon rolls, which only makes us more curious. How *do* the Denver City Council members eat their cinnamon rolls? Do they ingest them like normal people? Or do they do it in some odd way?

Citizens of Denver, we think you have the right to know how your elected officials consume their hot, glazed treats. But we cannot fight this fight for you. This is one struggle you must fight on your own. Hit the doughnut shop first.

Source: Associated Press

HISTORICAL DUMBOSITY: THE ZIMMERMANN TELEGRAM

World War I is the setting for perhaps the single greatest diplomatic blunder in history: the Zimmermann Telegram. Let's set the scene: It's early 1917, and the Germans and their allies have been fighting the French and English (and just about everyone else in Europe, with Canada and Japan tossed in for fun) for a good three years. The United States has been sitting out this little squabble, much to the despair of Great Britain, which is bleeding to death financially and has limited military resources. Germany knows that if the Americans enter the war, it'll be on the British side, and that'll be no good for the Kaiser. It's in Germany's interest to keep America neutral for as long as humanly possible.

Meet the Mastermind

Enter Arthur Zimmermann, Germany's foreign minister. Zimmermann decided that if the U.S. wouldn't stay neutral, then he should distract it. His strategy: an attack by Mexico! His plan was to convince Mexico that what it really wanted to do was start a border war with its northern neighbor. The U.S. would be so busy defending the Rio Grande that it wouldn't be able to get troops "over there." Somehow, in all the excitement, Japan, then currently allied with Great Britain, would change sides just for the fun of it and attack the U.S., too! What a swell plan!

The Logistics

Of course, Zimmermann didn't expect Mexico to attack the U.S. out of the kindness of its own heart. Germany would kick in cash to outfit the Mexicans and, when all was said and done, Mexico could have back the territory it lost to the U.S. You know: Texas, New Mexico, Arizona, and stuff like that. The U.S. would hardly miss 'em. It was a fine plan; now all Zimmermann had to do was tell Mexico about it.

He decided that the best way to get his message to Mexico was to go to the American embassy in Berlin and use its telegraph to send the message (encrypted, of course) to the German ambassador to the United States, who would then forward the message to Mexico. Now, you might think that using a U.S. telegraph line to send a message proposing an attack on the U.S. is a really dumb thing to do, and you'd be right. But probably not because of the reason you might suspect, which would be that the U.S. would somehow intercept the message. In fact, the U.S. was blissfully clueless about the content of the message it was sending down the line.

The British Wiles

No, it was stupid because the telegraph cable that went from Germany to the United States went through Great Britain—and the British had the line tapped. And not only did the British have the line tapped, they had also cracked the German military code, primarily through the British Navy stealing German code books from German ships they had sunk. This meant that the British could read

Zimmermann's encrypted message to the German ambassador—indeed, could read it more quickly than most German coded messages, since most German messages were encoded twice. Zimmermann's was encoded only once.

The German Soft Spot

Why didn't Zimmermann stop to consider that the telegraph line might be tapped, or that the German codes might be compromised? Zimmermann simply assumed that the German codes were so clever that they couldn't be cracked. And when they *were* cracked, he chalked it up to German carelessness— someone must have left a decoded version lying around. This same sort of arrogance would help the British 30 years later during World War II, when the Brits cracked the famous Enigma code and thus kept a critical intelligence edge over the Nazis. Thank God some people never learn.

The American Dilemma

But let's not get ahead of ourselves. Back in 1917, the British decoded the Zimmermann message and gave it Woodrow Wilson, the American president. Up to this point, Wilson had been fighting a rear-guard battle to keep the U.S. out of the war, but the idea of Germany negotiating with Mexico to carve up the U.S. like a Thanksgiving turkey really changed the climate. On March 1, 1917, American newspapers got hold of the telegram and predictably went nuts. Americans from coast to coast (and one suspects, especially in Texas, Arizona, and New Mexico) were outraged and spoiling to chuck the whole neutrality thing and kick some German tail.

But there still was an out: if Germany said that the telegram was a fake, everyone would be willing to forget it happened. Sure, the U.S. public was all riled up, but they could be toweled off and calmed down. Everybody could just step away from the diplomatic powder keg, leaving it unsparked and unexploded.

The Mastermind Strikes Again

So, of course, Zimmermann strolled in with a Molotov cocktail and threw it right on the powder. In one of the most mind-boggling diplomatic screw-ups in the history of man, Zimmermann refused to deny he'd written the telegram. "How can I?" he said. "It is true." In one sense it's admirable that, like George Washington, Zimmermann could not tell a lie. But in doing so, he also doomed Germany to defeat, which was probably not what he intended. The United States declared war against Germany in April 1917; in November 1918, World War I was over and Germany was hammered flat by the Treaty of Versailles. In all, not a real smooth move by Arthur Zimmermann.

And what of Mexico, you ask? Well, perhaps it recalled that the last time it went up against the U.S. it ended up forking over two-thirds of its land. A similar arrangement after another war might leave it with the Yucatan peninsula and not much else. Mexico politely declined Germany's offer of an alliance, suggesting blandly that the "premature publication" of the Zimmermann telegram made such an alliance politically disadvantageous. That's one way of putting it.

* * *

LET'S LEAVE HITLER OUT OF IT

Glenview State Bank of Illinois apologized to its customers after a newsletter observed that among the world leaders of the Depression-laden 1930s, Hitler alone presided over an expanding economy: "If we can understand why Depression-era Germany resisted the disease, we may better understand how alarmed we should be today in the 21st century," it read. Needless to say, the Anti-Defamation League was all over this baby nearly instantly, and the bank hastily retracted all claims of Hitler's economic genius.

Source: *Chicago Sun-Times*

* * *

"There is no sin except stupidity."

—Oscar Wilde

"It is only governments that are stupid, not the masses of people."

—Dwight D. Eisenhower

"Success in almost any field depends more on energy and drive than it does on intelligence. This explains why we have so many stupid leaders."

—Sloan Wilson

A COMBUSTIBLE SITUATION

Surely "Stanley" knew the police were coming for him. After all, when you spend your day (allegedly) harassing a woman with a hammer, crowbar, and rock, and then attempt some property damage on her house, you've pretty much put yourself on that day's police list of "People Who Should Be Cuffed and Read Their Rights."

But Stanley wasn't in the mood to interact in a positive manner with the local law enforcement of Gillette, Wyoming. So when the police showed up to give Stan an all-expenses-paid trip to the station, he countered with his own offer. He crawled underneath a nearby car, punctured the gas tank with a pen knife, and then declared that if the police got near him, he'd set the car on fire. And then, apparently just to prove that he was serious, he lit himself on fire, using a cigarette lighter to light up his gasoline-soaked clothes.

Burning with Bad Intentions

You can see the flaw in the plan here. To be honest, the plan was bad to begin with. Sure, threatening to blow up the car should have kept the cops at a distance, but then what? It's not like the cops would *leave*. And Stan couldn't spend the rest of his life prone beneath the wheels of someone else's automobile. But when you light *yourself* on fire, you know the cops aren't going to idly stand by. It's behavior that practically begs the police to intervene.

Once Stan inflamed himself, the cops ran in,

pulled him out from under the car, put him out, and arrested him on suspicion of aggravated assault and battery and third-degree arson. Looks like he got that all-expenses-paid trip down to the police station after all.

Source: Associated Press

* * *

DON'T TAKE THE CAR!

The first time the German three-year-old got behind the wheel, it was something of a fluke: he took the keys to the car, stuck them into ignition and drove about 10 yards before crashing the car. The kid was fine, but the car suffered about $5,000 in damage.

But there's no excuse for the second incident: a TV crew came to do a story about the kid, and they placed him in the car for a shot. When they weren't looking, the kid started the car and drove off again—crashing into another car and causing another $1,200 or so in damages. And he escaped unhurt again, thank goodness. Someone hide the keys already.

Source: Ananova

A POWERFUL
CLERICAL ERROR

Remember that time you accidentally transposed columns in a spreadsheet program and then when you printed out your report it said that your company had spent $100,000 on staples? Didn't you feel like a first-class moron? Well, relax. The guys at TransAlta Corp have you beat.

TransAlta is Canada's largest private power producer and wholesale power marketing company, with over $6 billion in assets, including coal-fired, gas-fired, hydro-fueled, and renewable power plants. You name it, TransAlta wrenches power from it. One of the things it does is to bid on energy contracts, like it did in May 2003, when it bid on transmission congestion contracts from the New York Independent System Operator. This sort of contract lets the state of New York keep power costs from spiraling madly out of control when there's a power crunch, and power providers bid on them regularly.

They Don't Excel at Proofreading

In the process of putting together its bids for the contracts, someone at TransAlta put the wrong information in the wrong place in an Excel spreadsheet. "It was literally a cut-and-paste error," TransAlta president Steve Snyder later told analysts. What this cut-and-paste error did was signal to the state of New York that TransAlta wanted to buy fifteen times the number of contracts it really wanted to buy, all at a higher price than it wanted to pay. Before TransAlta caught the error, the bids were accepted, and apparently in the high-stakes world of power management, there is no such thing as a do-over.

The cost to TransAlta for this spreadsheet error? $24 million dollars, and that's in U.S. and not Canadian dollars. That's a lot of staples.

Sources: *Toronto Globe & Mail*, Canadian Press

* * *

GIVE ME YOUR TIRED, HUNGRY, AND MILDLY OBESE

A Venezuelan woman filed for political asylum in Canada on the grounds that if she were to return to her home country, people would make fun of her because she was fat. Citizenship and Immigration Canada declined her application because, among other things, "at the hearing, the claimant did not appear to fit the dictionary definition of obese." Meanwhile, a spokesperson for Venezuela's Canadian embassy denied chubby women were persecuted in that country. "My mother is overweight and she is very happy," the spokesperson said.

Source: *National Post* (Canada)

COURT ORDER: DECEASED SPOUSE MUST PAY ALIMONY

In May 2003, an appeals court in Boston ruled that an ex-husband had to continue paying alimony to his ex-wife despite the interesting mitigating circumstance that he'd been dead for five years.

But Is It Legal? You Bet!

The reason? The wording of the alimony agreement between the former married couple. In general, once you're dead, you're relieved of any additional need to pay alimony (or, for that matter, to pay for anything). However, in the agreement, our husband agreed to pay alimony until the "death or remarriage" of his spouse. In other words, all it said was that the ex-wife had to die or remarry to stop getting alimony. It never specified that the ex-husband had to remain living to pay it.

The lawyers for the estate of the ex-husband maintained that the wording was ambiguous and that the ex-husband never intended to keep paying alimony after he died. But the appeals court found no ambiguity in the agreement. Justice Mel Greenberg wrote, "[The ex-wife] has neither died nor remarried, and therefore [the ex-husband's] estate is bound to continue making payments."

So let that be a warning to all you would-be-bitter ex-husbands: Remember to specify "Till Death Do We Part." Even after the divorce.

Source: *Boston Herald*

HARRY POTTER AND THE REALITY-IMPAIRED FAN

Now, we love those Harry Potter books just as much as anyone. But while we enjoy the adventures of Harry, Ron, Hermione, and everyone else loitering around Hogwart's, we always keep a grip on one unassailable fact: it's all fictional. This is why we don't hurl ourselves out of a second-story window, riding a broom and looking for other wizards to participate in a quick pickup game of Quidditch. As appealing as the idea may be, the real world (and the force of gravity therein) would quickly assert itself.

Would that "Eva" had clearly delineated the realms of fantasy and reality, but the 21-year-old native of Madrid had not. Armed with "wizardry" she would later claim was inspired by the Potter books, Eva decided she would make a magic potion. And so she set to work, mixing olive oil, rubbing alcohol, and toothpaste together. She put it on the stove to cook it and waited for something spectacular to happen.

And something did: Eva's magic potion burst into flames, which spread to the rest of her home. Eva had to be treated at the scene for smoke inhalation.

All in all, not a very magical moment for Eva.

Source: Ananova

AND IOWA'S STREETS WILL FLOW CORNHUSKER RED!

The last time American states went to war, hundreds of thousands died on both sides, brother fought brother, Atlanta burned, and Scarlett went hungry. So interstate warfare is not something one enters into lightly. It's better to let state rivalries be fought the way they've been for over a century now: on the football field. Heck, it's kept Ohio and Michigan from annihilating each other for decades.

But some people just aren't satisfied with long bombs that involve a pigskin. They wanted real war. Take Nebraska senator Pam Brown of Omaha. In May 2003, Senator Brown tried to convince her colleagues that what Nebraska needed was some major combat with neighboring Iowa. She introduced a piece of legislation that declared "a state of hostility with the sovereign state of Iowa until such a time as the state of Iowa ceases the unjust and relentless appropriation of the resources of the citizens of Nebraska."

Iowa Is the Favorite

A case of cross-border cow-snatching or cornfield razing? Nothing so agricultural. Seems that Nebraskans like gambling and they can't legally do it in Nebraska. So they cross the border into Iowa, which allows gambling, and spend a whole bunch of cash that Senator Brown thinks should be spent in the home state. How much? An estimated $250 million a year at the Council Bluff casinos, which are located, mockingly, right across the border from Senator Brown's Omaha. Interestingly, the declaration of war was attached as a rider on a proposed constitutional amendment that would allow gambling in Nebraska.

There are a couple of roadblocks to Nebraska going to war against Iowa, primarily that the U.S. constitution doesn't allow individual states to take up arms against each other. Yes, yes, the Civil War, but that was *absolutely the last time*, kids.

Anyway, Senator Brown later rescinded her proposed declaration of war. Iowans from Des Moines to Ottumwa can sleep safe, knowing their borders are safe from rampaging Cornhusker militias.

Of course, that's just what the Nebraskans want the Iowans to think.

Source: Associated Press

* * *

"Johnson having argued for some time with a pertinacious gentleman; his opponent, who had talked in a very puzzling manner, happened to say, 'I don't understand you, Sir'; upon which Johnson observed, 'Sir, I have found you an argument; but I am not obliged to find you an understanding.'"

—James Boswell

BABY, YOU CAN DRIVE
MY CAR—IN SEVEN YEARS

When reading this story, give "Otto," our hero, this much credit: he knew he was too drunk to drive. When it came time to go, Otto took a moment of (relatively) sober reflection and realized that more people than just himself would be at risk if he got behind the wheel. So let it be noted that Otto chose not to drive drunk. In the moment of truth, he took his keys and handed them to his friend "Susie" and told her to drive.

Too bad she was nine years old.

While Susie was behind the wheel, Otto's car veered off the road and hit a tent at a campground in Moses Lake, Washington. Unfortunately, there were people in the tent at the time; two were injured but fortunately were expected to make a full recovery.

Meanwhile, Otto is in trouble with the Grant County sheriff's office. True enough, he didn't drink and drive. But handing the keys to someone whose entire driving experience up to that point may have consisted of pushing along her Malibu Barbie Corvette really isn't any better. Friends don't let friends drive drunk—or prepubescently.

Source: Associated Press

* * *

"The older I grow, the more I distrust the familiar doctrine that age brings wisdom."

—H. L. Mencken

AND HERE I THOUGHT GUTVIK WAS A KIND OF FISH

I KEA, the Swedish furniture giant, is known for affordable, stylish pieces that can be assembled at home with a single freakish tool. It's also known for giving each of its products a Scandinavian name. From the Albäck solid birch hat and coat stand ("Eighteen knobs in different heights make it useful for everyone") to the Wicke computer desk (with swing-out mouse shelf and optional drapes to hide your workspace), everything IKEA sells has a name that's often amusingly unpronounceable and which you will undoubtedly forget the moment you get the thing home.

Just Put Glimma on the Duvemar

Sometimes a word IKEA uses to describe a product will resemble words in other languages like Bar magnets (which are not actually bar magnets), Curry chairs, and the Flabb wall lamp. Other names are not real words in English but are snigger-worthy if you have an infantile mind (for example, the Beslut conference chair or the Diktad line of furnishings), which makes one wonder how carefully the IKEA head office pays attention to how the names might translate in other places.

Gutvik? I'll Take Two!

Evidence that IKEA *doesn't* pay much attention to how the names might translate came in April 2003 when it put the Gutvik bunk beds on sale across Europe. IKEA maintains that the word is the name of a small town in Sweden (the town is actually in Norway, 330 kilometers from Trondheim). But as it happens, it's also a slang word in Germany, where it means "good f***."

By the time someone pointed this out to the IKEA folks, ads for the beds had been printed up, sent out to newspapers, and plastered on windows. The ads, as you might imagine, were hastily withdrawn.

However, interestingly enough, as of this writing the Gutvik bunk beds are still on sale on the German IKEA Web site. As they might say in Sweden, whööps.

Source: Ananova

* * *

ON SOLID GROUNDS

A Romanian woman asked for a divorce from her husband on the grounds that the man kept calling out the name of his first wife while he slept—every night for the three months since they had been married. "How could I live with a man who sleeps besides me but has sex with the ex-wife in his dreams?" she asked the court. Well, it is marginally better than the other way around.

Source: Ananova

TIPS FOR STUPID CRIMINALS

Welcome to Tips for Stupid Criminals! Because, let's be honest, stupid criminals need all the tips they can get.

YOU LOOK AWFULLY FAMILIAR
Today's tip: When handing a stolen ID to a store clerk to cash a stolen check, make sure the person on the ID is not the store clerk in question.

Seems that down in sultry Louisiana, a store clerk was visiting a friend in Metaire when her car was broken into and her purse was stolen, along with her checkbook, ID, and other objects typically tucked away in a purse. A week later, our clerk had just punched in to work when her first customer in line wrote out a check for $259.17. The clerk thought the checkbook looked familiar and the check even more so. Perhaps it was the Looney Tunes characters on the checks that were the giveaway, or else it was the clerk's own name on the check. Either way, the clerk asked for ID and was handed her own, recently stolen driver's license. "I still don't know how she didn't realize it was me," the clerk told a reporter. Further examination of the customer's purse after her arrest netted ID cards from five other women. It's unknown if any of them were store clerks as well.

Source: *New Orleans Times-Picayune*

THE REALLY STUPID QUIZ: ESCAPED PRISONERS

Put on your thinking caps, because it's time for a Really Stupid Quiz. In this quiz (and others like it throughout the book, you'll be presented with three news stories. One of them is true; two of them are false. All of them feature someone doing something really stupid. Your job: decide which one of the three is really stupid (i.e., actually happened). Think it's going to be easy? Guess again.

1. A German criminal who had escaped from a city jail in Hamburg was rearrested after he posted an online personal ad admitting he was an escaped felon. On the German version of Yahoo! Personals, he wrote, "In the spirit of openness, I have to say I have a criminal past and I am hiding from police as I have escaped from jail. But I am looking forward to turning over a new leaf with the right woman." Yahoo! staff notified police, and an undercover officer, who posed as a woman looking to meet a match, arrested the criminal as he waited for his "date" at a café in Bremen.

2. An escapee from a São Paulo, Brazil, prison was rearrested on his first day at his new job—as a bus driver taking friends and relatives to visit prisoners at another São Paulo prison. How the escaped prisoner got the job in the first place is still a mystery, but he was taken into custody after a routine inspection disclosed his true identity. Said a police spokesperson: "How dumb can you be? You escape

prison and then get a job where you drive inside another prison every week?"

3. A prisoner who had been serving time for arson escaped from a state penitentiary in Nevada and attempted to hitch a ride on a highway by displaying a sign that read "Just Escaped from Prision [sic]—Give a Guy a Break!" And in fact it worked, up to a point: a truck driver picked him up and drove him to the next truck stop on the highway. He bought the escapee breakfast and encouraged him to take a shower. While our escaped prisoner was showering, the trucker had the waitress contact the police, who rearrested the escapee as he was coming out of the shower.

Which one is really stupid?

Answer page 311.

Source: Ananova

* * *

NOTE TO ESCAPING PRISONERS

Watch where you're going. The *St. Louis Post-Dispatch* reported on a guest of the St. Charles County Jail who tried to make a break for it while being escorted back to his cell. Our man broke free from his escort, ran toward a fire exit and raced out of it—and smack into a concrete retaining wall about three feet from the door. The end result: a severe head injury and no escape. Ouch.

Source: *St. Louis Post-Dispatch*

YIPES! STRIPES!

The city burghers of Glassport, Pennsylvania, took a look around their governmental chambers in early May 2003 and decided that the place needed a good sprucing up. They didn't know how right they were until they discovered that the American flag that stood in the council chamber was out of date by over 40 years.

The flag in question had 48 stars on it, and had last accurately flown in 1959, the year Alaska became the 49th state (followed quickly by Hawaii). Apparently no one noticed the flag was out of date because it was draped around a flag stand—for *44 years*. It hadn't been touched since the Eisenhower administration.

Local congressman Mike Doyle helped bring the government of Glassport into the 21st century by donating an updated American flag. Other suggested donation items for our time travelers: a couple of Beatles albums, a "Have a Nice Day" button, a Rubik's Cube, and a Tamagotchi.

Source: Associated Press

* * *

"I like to think of my behavior in the '60s as a 'learning experience.' Then again, I like to think of anything stupid I've done as a 'learning experience.' It makes me feel less stupid."

—P. J. O'Rourke

ONE MORE ITEM FOR THE "DO NOT PLACE IN MICROWAVE LIST"

Everybody loves a money-saving beauty tip. The staff of Argentina's *Claudia* magazine had a good one—if you just heated your dried-out nail polish in the microwave for three minutes, it would be good as new.

Who doesn't like good as new? Certainly not thrifty Argentinean ladies! All over the great South American country, women tossed polish into microwaves and zapped the bottles for the same length of time as you'd zap a microwavable mini pizza.

Sadly, it appears the staff at *Claudia* magazine did not field-test the tip in their own microwaves, or they might have known that in many cases, the combination of nail polish and microwave radiation equals an exploding microwave. More than 100 readers of *Claudia*, however, did try this tip and were rewarded, not with rejuvenated polish but with wrecked household appliances. The staff at *Claudia* was forced to publish an apology.

One would hope they also sent those women some new nail polish. At the *very* least.

Source: Ananova

NOT WHAT IS USUALLY MEANT BY "MIXED MEDIA"

A recipe for trouble: one modern-art museum, ten blenders filled with water, no less than ten goldfish in said water in said blenders, and at least one sadistic art lover.

Mix all four ingredients together and what you'll get is probably very similar to what happened at the Trapholt Art Museum in Kolding, Denmark, in early 2000. The museum was hosting an installation by artist Marco Evaristti, which featured working blenders with goldfish in them, and an invitation to visitors to go ahead and grind up the little fishies if that's what they really wanted to do.

Well, at least one person did, and two of the goldfish found themselves blended (or, depending on the blender setting, whipped, crushed, or frappéed) into oblivion. The art museum isn't sure who the person was, but here's a tip: look back through the records to find if a high school class had a field trip that day. Call it a feeling.

Cruel and Unusual
Speaking of feeling, animal rights activists felt the installation was cruel to the goldfish. The Kolding police agreed and fined museum director Peter Meyer the equivalent of $315. Meyer refused to pay, contending that being killed by whirling blades wasn't in the least bit cruel, a point of view which, if nothing else, makes us want to be sure not to let Mr. Meyer

anywhere near our home aquariums. Everyone went off to court, except for the goldfish.

The wheels of justice in Denmark move considerably more slowly than the blades of death, and it wasn't until May 2003 that Judge Preben Bagger announced his ruling and sided with Meyer, saying the fish had died instantly (which was probably true) and humanely. Bagger was guided in his decision in part by a representative of blender manufacturer Moulinex, who in expert witness testimony maintained the fish would have been thoroughly blended within a second. And maybe so.

Source: Associated Press

* * *

TREE HUGGER, TREE KILLER

Now, this has got to be embarrassing . . . A prominent environmental activist admitted to violating state timber harvest rules when he chopped down trees on his land to make way for his new home—creating potential harm to the habitat of the red tree vole and the coast lily, two closely watched California species. The employee, who spearheaded efforts to stop logging in the Jackson State Forest, swore it was "an inadvertent violation of the law . . . There was no real harm done."

Hey, tell it to the red tree vole!

Source: Associated Press

UP IN SMOKE

Nobody likes mosquitoes, but some like them less than others. Like "Joao," a citizen of mosquito-laden Dourados, Brazil. Joao was upset by the fact that the small bloodsuckers had invaded his home, and he resolved to eradicate the little vampires.

There are a number of ways to dispatch mosquitoes, although each has its disadvantages. Flyswatters work, but it is time-consuming to go after the mosquitoes one at a time. Citronella candles bother mosquitoes, but they smell funny. Bats feast on the insects, but an echolocating flying mammal just doesn't go with most interior decor.

Like a House Afire

We don't know how many mosquito-eradicating options Joao considered. We only know which one he took: he set a piece of paper on fire and used it to scare off the bugs. Unfortunately, the fire got out of hand. First the room Joao was in, and then his entire house, was engulfed in crackling, mosquito-scaring flames. Joao's neighbors, no less scared, called the fire brigade.

As his house burned down, Joao remained admirably focused. "When we took him out he was still angry about the mosquitoes and kept asking if they were gone," said a member of the fire brigade.

Next up: Joao removes a fly from his own forehead. Ambulances are standing by.

Sources: Ananova, *Terra Noticias Populares*

TIPS FOR STUPID CRIMINALS

Because stupid criminals might make smart readers.

TOOL TIME
Today's tip: It's bad form to look for a job at the same place you recently robbed.

I ronically, the reason "Art" robbed that construction company in Stillwater, Oklahoma, seems to be that when he went there looking for a job in June 2003, no one was around. And perhaps Art figured, heck, there's no reason why he should have come all that way for *nothing*. Whatever Art's thought processes (or lack thereof), he came away from that construction site with a power tool and several goodies he lifted from a car on the site.

Unbeknownst to Art, his adventures in thievery were recorded on a security camera. And so, when he came back to the construction company the next day, employees recognized him as they guy who'd helped himself to whatever wasn't pinned down the day before. The folks at the company kept him on the premises by interviewing him for a job; while he was talking about his qualifications, the cops showed up and hauled him away.

Art didn't get a second interview. Apparently they don't give points for initiative. Or audacity.

Source: Reuters

DUMB MOVIE FESTIVAL: KANGAROO JACK (2003)

Our Entry: *Kangaroo Jack,* starring Jerry O'Connell and Anthony Anderson

The Plot (Such As It Is): Two witless mob couriers (O'Connell and Anderson) travel to Australia (accompanied by many utterances of "G'day" and Men at Work tunes) where they promptly lose $50,000 of mob cash to a computer-generated kangaroo. Thenceforth follows a chase across the continent with O'Connell and Anderson being outsmarted by the kangaroo every step of the way.

Superhot model Estella Warren shows up as a naturalist primarily to give the targeted nine-year-old male audience a head start on hormonal urges. Despite being presented as a kid's film, the flick is full of adult-style violence and groping. Produced by Jerry Bruckheimer, known for super-violent, super-dumb action films.

Fun Fact: Cowritten by Steve Bing, better known to most of the world for being the guy who denied impregnation of Elizabeth Hurley. He owned up to this, however. Odd value system, there, Steve.

Total North American Box Office: $66,723,216 (source: The-Numbers.com). Yes, it was actually a hit. Weep for civilization.

The Critics Rave!

"Virtually every shot of the kangaroo was digitally created, and perhaps that was an insurance policy masterstroke. Forcing a real live one to act opposite these co-stars could have easily constituted animal cruelty."—*Village Voice*

"I couldn't find a plot here with a gun to my head, but it has something to do with a white hairdresser, a black street hustler and a kangaroo named Jack. A reward is promised if you can tell them apart . . . I've had more laughs and bigger thrills in a petting zoo."—*New York Observer*

"My four-year-old nephew can write his own name. This puts him several steps above the folks who wrote the screenplay for *Kangaroo Jack* . . . O'Connell and Anderson have all the comic instincts of Leopold and Loeb."—Nitrate Online

"It's a scientific fact that nothing hits the sweet spot of your average 10-year-old kid like the sight of a kangaroo in a red Brooklyn jacket and sunglasses boogieing down to 'the hip, hop, the hippety-hop.' The more pressing question is: Will parents be able to sit through *Kangaroo Jack* without plunging sharp sticks into their eyes?"—*Boston Globe*

"Why there is a genuinely menacing gangster subplot in what advertises itself as a lighthearted family entertainment (overlooking the alcohol abuse, women-bashing, casual indifference to the law, beating of old men, and uncomfortable racial dynamic) is a problem that comments not only on the fact that *Kangaroo Jack* probably began life as an adult entertainment, but highlights the alien-ness of the kangaroo foolishness in the proceedings."—Film Freak Central

"I'm not sure which news is more distressing, that this movie cost $65,000,000 to make or that it took in over $67,000,000 in box office receipts."—DVD Town

THE REALLY STUPID QUIZ:
WACKY WORLD LEADERS

Time for another Really Stupid Quiz! Remember: one of these stories is true. Two of them are false. All are stupid. You decide which seems more realistically stupid to you.

1. Fun-loving Fidel Castro pulled a fast one on Venezuelan president Hugo Chavez when the two of them were in Paraguay for the swearing in of that country's new president. Castro convinced a Paraguayan minister of parliament to warn Chavez about a possible ambush, and when Chavez walked through a doorway, Castro jumped out at him from behind the door, badly startling his fellow head of state. Later, Chavez said it was just "a joke amongst friends."

2. Cherie Blair, the wife of British prime minister Tony Blair, was offered a recording contract by Madonna's Maverick Records after a cheeky club remix of Mrs. Blair singing the Beatles song "When I'm 64" became a surprise hit in the U.K. and Spain. "The idea would be to have her sing some classic tunes and do some spoken word bits, like that "Everybody's Free (to Wear Sunscreen)" hit Baz Luhrmann had a few years ago," a Maverick Records executive said. Mrs. Blair reportedly turned down the offer, citing other commitments and a desire to avoid conflicts with her husband's job.

3. President Arnold Ruutel of Estonia had an emergency trip to a Tallinn hospital when a comedy skit for

Estonia's popular "Everybody's Laughing" TV show
went awry. In the skit, Ruutel sat for a mock press conference (during which he jokingly declared war on
neighbors Finland and Latvia) and at the end was
smacked in the face with a pie by the show's host. Some
of the pie filling worked its way underneath one of
Ruutel's contact lenses, abrading his cornea and necessi-
tating a hospital visit. Damage was minor, although
doctors made Ruutel wear an eye patch for a week. At
a real press conference the next day, Ruutel laughingly
announced his retirement from show business.

Which one is really stupid?

Answer page 311.

Source: Ananova

* * *

"Only in Britain could it be thought a defect to be 'too
clever by half.' The probability is that too many people
are too stupid by three-quarters."

—John Major

"I've had a lot of experience with people smarter than
I am."

—Gerald Ford

"So dumb he can't fart and chew gum at the same
time."

—Lyndon B. Johnson, speaking of Gerald Ford

MONEY FOR NOTHING

Here's another pop quiz for you. You go to your ATM to take out some money. Upon receiving your money, you take your receipt and see that your cash balance is $500,418.02, which is roughly half a million more than you were aware you had. What do you do next? a) go to the bank to let someone know about the error, or b) engage in a mad rush to spend as much of it as humanly possible before the bank catches the error?

If your answer tends more toward the second option than the first, let us delight you with the cautionary tale of "Darren," of Ogden, Utah. In July 2003, a Denver title company wired some money to a bank account, and accidentally punched in the wrong account number. Presto, a cool half million magically appeared in Darren's bank account. And Darren allegedly did something he shouldn't have; he started spending that half million. He bought three cars, for a grand total of $116,000. He spent another $114,000 on miscellaneous stuff.

Thing is: just because some money is in your bank account doesn't mean it's *yours*. And sooner or later the people who it belongs to are going to want it back, and they're likely to ask for the help of local, state and federal authorities. Which is exactly what happened in this case: the cops finally caught up with Darren in Salt Lake City and arrested him on the charge of felony theft, which is what it's called when you spend $230,000 that's not yours. The cars?

Impounded. Let's hope it was fun while it lasted.

The moral: Free money isn't free. Darren's probably going to be paying for his for a while.

Source: Associated Press

* * *

I'M APPLYING FOR THE
POSITION OF BANK ROBBER

"Albert" had a lovely résumé—too bad he wrote a bomb threat on the back of it. Al used the résumé and the bomb threat to rob a Fort Worth, Texas, bank. Once he got the cash, he fled the scene, foolishly leaving the résumé behind. He'd covered up the personal information by taping paper over it, but let's suggest that tape is easily dealt with. As was Albert, who was nabbed soon after.

Source: *Fort Worth Star-Telegram*

* * *

"Most fools think they are only ignorant."

—Benjamin Franklin

THE HIGH COST OF SITTING

You see a bench at a park, you figure, that's someplace I can sit. After all, that's what benches are designed for. Unless you tried to sit on a certain bench in the Botanical Gardens in Munich, as "Rolf" found out.

While strolling the gardens, which he intended to revisit with his kid later that week, Rolf took at a seat on a bench near a playground. Suddenly—police! Of all the benches in all the botanical gardens in the world, it seemed that this was the one that you couldn't sit on.

Arrested for Resting

The reason—it was next to a playground, and adults weren't allowed to sit there unless accompanied by a child. The regulation was to make sure kids weren't harassed by creepy lowlifes who like to hang out in parks. Fair enough, but as Rolf noted later to the *Sueddeutsche Zeitung* newspaper, there were no kids in the playground. He was just resting his feet.

It didn't matter: he came away with a fine of 150 euros (about $150). At his court date, the judge compromised and let Rolf donate 75 euros to charity, but no matter how you look it, that's a lot of cash for the simple act of sitting down. So be careful where you sit at the Munich Botanical Gardens. But don't blame the bench—it's not the bench's fault.

Source: Ananova

A STUPID EXCUSE
THAT WASN'T

In the mood for a refreshing change of pace? Here
we have a story of a stupid excuse that wasn't. It's
got everything: Drama! Accusations! Redemption!
And burritos. Especially burritos.

Our story begins with Adam of Nebraska. Adam
was serving a 364-day sentence for driving with a suspended license, but he was allowed to work in the real
world during the day. One day after work, Adam tested
out with a low level of alcohol in his system, which
was a violation of his work-release agreement. Wham,
he's in court, and the prosecutors are accusing him of
knocking back a few during the work day.

But Adam had an excuse: it was the burritos. It
seems that one of his coworkers had brought in burritos
made with meat that had been soaked in alcohol before
it was cooked. Adam, apparently a man of prodigious
appetites, claimed to have eaten four of these burritos,
and *that*, he claimed, was what was responsible for the
alcohol. Yeah, *that's* it.

Fine, said Lincoln County district judge John
Murphy. Bring me the recipe. And a burrito.

Exhibit B for Burrito
Adam *did*. At the next court hearing, he presented
Murphy with the recipe for the burritos, a recipe that
called for one bottle of red Irish beer, 1 1/2 cups of
tequila and three-quarters of a bottle of dark ale. That's
some very drunken meat. And Murphy agreed, even to

the point of forgoing chowing down on the burrito itself. "It is unnecessary to conduct a taste test of the burritos," Murphy wrote in his ruling. "The list of ingredients indicates that there is sufficient alcohol in the burritos for a preliminary breath test to register positive."

Also, Murphy noted, the utter ridiculousness of Adam's "It was the burrito!" excuse ultimately worked in his favor. "No rational person would use a 'burrito' defense as a means of covering up the consumption of alcohol during a period of work release," he wrote. This is, we think, an excellent point. So congratulations, Adam. The truth is stranger than stupidity.

And now we're really in the mood for burritos. What was that recipe again?

Source: Associated Press

* * *

DUBIOUS ACHIEVEMENT IN ALCOHOL

German police pulled over a man who was driving erratically and ordered him out of his car to administer a sobriety test. When the man exited the car, so did his dog, a West Highland white terrier. As the police gave the man commands for the sobriety test, the dog performed them as well. The man failed the test. The dog, on the other hand, performed all the commands flawlessly, including a 360 degree turn, which caused the man to fall. Left unanswered, of course, is who trains his dog to pass a sobriety test?

Source: Reuters

THE HURTINGEST MAN IN THE WORLD

Depending on who you are, this is a story that is either too sad for words or a prime example of how the karmic boomerang will come back and bash you right across the face the very first chance it gets. Only you can decide which group you belong to.

Our tragic hero/karmic-boomerang victim is "Otto," a disabled man living in the city of Tilburg, in the Netherlands. Otto discovered somewhere along the way that sex helped to ease his pain without medication. So, he figured, the local municipal council should grant him a monthly sex allowance, for its healing medicinal properties.

Not Your Father's HMO

Now, this might seem like a profoundly wacky idea, especially to Americans. But in the Netherlands you can walk down certain streets and see women in windows posing in lingerie—and they're not selling nighties. So Otto actually got a judge to buy his line of reasoning, and in 1997, after a seven-year legal struggle, Otto's local government was ordered to shell out the equivalent of about $125 a month for Otto's sexual healing.

Let's Do It Under the Table

Ah, but here's where the karmic boomerang comes around for the smackdown. In August 2003, *De Telegraaf* reported that Otto was having an extremely difficult time with his "therapy." It's not that prostitutes were hard to find, it's just that none of them was willing to give Otto a receipt, which he requires in order to get reimbursed for his adventures. You see, if prostitutes provide a receipt, then the income is taxable, because the government has a record of (ahem) "services rendered." Prostitutes, who are in it for the money, prefer whenever possible not to split that money with the government.

So that creates an interesting catch-22 for Otto: the government pays for his sex, but because the government pays for his sex, he can't get any. That karmic boomerang, it's a painful thing.

Sources: Expatica.com, *De Telegraaf*

* * *

HAVING HIS "MAN CARD" REVOKED

A Croatian man really didn't want to have sex with wife, and apparently the excuse of having a headache just wouldn't work. So he tried something else to avoid his connubial duty—he set fire to the woods behind his house. It worked, in that he and the wife had to be evacuated from the house while firefighters tended to the blaze. But then he also had to go to jail. Hey, that gets him out of having sex, too.

Source: Ananova

A CHEESY AIRPORT SECURITY STORY

Okay, these days it's not a bad idea for the security guys at the airport to be a little paranoid about everything. Why? Well, as just one example, as we were getting ready to write up this particular piece for the book, CNN was blaring out a story of a nine-year-old's teddy bear that went through an airport scanner with a loaded pistol tucked inside its adorably cuddly belly. The kid said he had no idea how that gun got into the teddy bear; it'd been a gift from a girl he met at the hotel where his family had been vacationing. The point is paranoid airport security people have reason to be paranoid. That's okay by us.

Still, let's also admit there's a difference between nabbing a pistol-packin' plush toy and what happened to Norwegian-born Tore Fauske as he got ready to board a plane in Brussels for a trip back to England, where he resides.

What a Cheesy Gift!

While in Brussels for a business trip Fauske was presented with the Norwegian delicacy *geitost* (it's pronounced "yay-toast")—a type of goat cheese that the Web site Cheese.com assures us has a "sweet, fishy, caramel flavor that is really irresistible." (We're pretty sure that any food that is described as tasting both of fish and of caramel is something we could resist, yeah, with a vengeance, even.)

Clearly Fauske did not have the same problem; he

happily received the cheese and stuffed it into his carry-on bag, which apparently didn't have anything in it that would suffer from smelling like fishy cheesy caramel after a long flight. Off he went to the security gates. As his carry-on went through the security checkpoint, a funny thing happened: Fauske was stopped and everyone behind him in line was shooed off to other checkpoints. Then security people asked Fauske to open his bag. "The guards visibly took a step backward when I unzipped it," he told the *Stavanger Aftenblad* newspaper.

An Unexplosive Situation

There sat the geitost, brown and hard and, clearly, suspected of being some sort of explosive device. (Which it might very well be if you're lactose intolerant.) Fauske tried to explain to the security guards what the substance was, but as you might imagine, anything smelling both of fish and caramel might not strike the uninitiated as edible. Eventually Fauske had to eat some in front of the guards. "It wasn't until I demonstrated that it clearly was something edible that they relaxed," he said.

The moral of the story: If the airport security guards are worried you might explode, don't be afraid to cut the cheese.

Sources: *Stavanger Aftenblad*, *Aftenposten* English Web Desk, Cheese.Com

CHICKEN LEGS! CHICKEN LEGS!

As you may or may not know, in the United States—the First Amendment notwithstanding—there are certain limits about what you can say regarding the sitting president of the United States. For example, if you say something threatening, you might get a visit from a couple of unsmiling Secret Service agents.

But what happens if you don't threaten the sitting president of the United States but merely suggest that he or she could, you know, stand to exercise a little more? Well in that case, you don't get visited by the Secret Service, but you might find yourself banned from a bookstore in Virginia. Which is what happened to singer/songwriter Julia Rose after a July 2003 appearance at a Fredericksburg, Virginia, bookstore.

Rose, who in addition to being a songwriter is also a notable fitness enthusiast, took a dim view of the lower appendages of President George W. Bush. She said of them: "George Bush has chicken legs. He needs to pump some iron." The line got some laughter, and then Rose went on with her set.

Afterward, however, she discovered that someone must have thought that describing the president's legs as resembling a chicken's was akin to passing along state secrets. She was informed that as a result of her comments she had been banned from further appearances at the local store. Store representatives refused to comment to the press as to why she was banned, although they noted that Rose could perform in the chain's other bookstores in the area—unless, said an area marketing manager, "I receive any more complaints."

"I never said anything about Bush being a bad president or anything," Rose told the Fredericksburg *Free Lance-Star*. "I was just poking fun at his scrawny frame." So for all you other singer/songwriters out there, just watch it when you poke fun at the president's legs, whomever he or she might be. And for God's sake, don't *actually* poke at his or her frame, for fun or any other reason. That will call the attention of the Secret Service.

Sources: Fredericksburg *Free Lance-Star*, Sunspot.net

* * *

A ONE AND A TWO . . .

Singer Dannii Minogue was performing a concert at the Kingsbury Water Park near Tamworth, England, when she noticed a boat sinking out in the water. She tried to alert the audience to the sinking boat by pointing to it while she sang, but the audience, thinking she was doing some zany new dance move, merely copied the singer's movements and started pointing back at her. "Every time she pointed out at us, we pointed back at her," one concertgoer said. Fortunately, the man on the boat was able to right the boat and return to safety.

Source: Ananova

HOW NOT TO
CLEANSE YOUR PALATE

Normally, when your waiter offers a round of schnapps on the house, it's a cause for celebration. But in Klagenfurt, Austria, it was the cause of something else: a trip to the emergency room.

The fun began when the waiter announced to the dinner party he was serving that they were getting a free round of schnapps. He took a bottle from behind the bar, poured for his guests, everyone toasted, and slugged back the schnapps. This was followed by the reddening of faces, the gasping of air, and some surprised coughing. In other words, your basic schnapps aftermath.

May We Suggest a Little Sorbet Instead?
But the basic schnapps aftermath didn't *stop*, and when they were able to speak again, the diners complained. The waiter, thinking either that he shouldn't serve anything he wouldn't consume himself, or just not hip to his patrons' obvious pain, poured himself a shot. Soon he was gasping, coughing, and choking just like his guests. Everyone went to the hospital, where they were treated for burns to the mouth and throat. They'd consumed detergent, which the bartender had poured into a schnapps bottle behind the bar. Clearly, the bartender hadn't alerted the wait staff. So the next time you're in Klagenfurt, Austria, and your waiter offers you a free drink, have him go first.

Source: Reuters

ANATOMY OF A DUMB EXCUSE: THE NEKKID PILOTS

Welcome to Anatomy of a Dumb Excuse, in which we show how someone perpetrating a really stupid maneuver just makes it worse by offering up an even stupider excuse.

Our Contestants: Two pilots, working for a national airline. Let's call them "Bob" and "Fred."

The Dumb Move: While piloting their 757, Bob and Fred are discovered by a flight attendant to have removed most or indeed all of their clothing (reports are sketchy on this point). They were subsequently dismissed by the airline due to "inappropriate conduct."

The Even Dumber Excuse: Bob and Fred contend that they removed their clothing because coffee spilled on one of them.

Why This Is a Dumb Excuse: "Coffee spilled on one of them." This is a fine excuse for the one who actually had the spill—Fred. Hot coffee equals third-degree burns, which equals painful gyrations, which could mean accidentally bumping into the flight yoke and plunging an airliner 4,000 feet in three seconds and plastering all the passengers onto the cabin roof. No one wants that. So, all right, fine, Fred's off the hook. *He's* got an excuse for taking off at least one article of clothing.

But then there's Bob. Bob had no free-flying

caffeinated beverage issues. He had no reason for taking off his tie, shirt, pants, and shoes, except possibly that he was performing a sympathy strip for Fred, so Fred wouldn't feel uncomfortable being naked in the cockpit. This impulse, while considerate, has its own psychological pathology that one hopes doesn't exist in the people who control a metal tube filled with other people, hurtling through the air at several hundred miles an hour, and at an altitude of 28,000 feet.

The Truth, As Far As We Can Tell

All told, it's better to think this was just a couple of guys, who happened to be pilots, doing something stupid. Really, who's gonna know they're naked and flying a plane? Perhaps *all* pilots do it when they think no one is looking. We don't know. And now that they've installed those secure cockpit doors, we may never be able to find out.

The airline itself seems to have given more credence to the "guys doing dumb things" idea—*USA Today*, which reported on the story, noted that the company was treating the incident as a "prank that went too far." Not too mention too high up in the air.

Sources: *USA Today*, CNN/Money.com

* * *

"One must be a little foolish, if one does not want to be even more stupid."

—Michel de Montaigne

ANOTHER THIRD
WILL HAVE TO SIT AT
THE NERD TABLE AT LUNCH

It's June 2003, and once again it's time for kindergarten graduation at Bangs Avenue Elementary School in Asbury Park, New Jersey. It was a tough year, what with all those nap and snack times, educational play, and being warned not to run with scissors, but darn it, the kids were up to it. Now, older and wiser, they head off to the verdant pastures of first grade, and then Harvard! (Or at least Rutgers.)

This year, it fell to the vice-principal of Bangs Elementary to make graduating remarks to the kids; you know, something to inspire them as they make their way into first grade, or perhaps a mild warning that while eating paste was cool in kindergarten, the sophisticated palates of upperclassmen stick to actual comestibles. In order were some nice and light comments to usher the tykes off to a summer of cartoons and water slides and sugary fruit-flavored drinks.

Why They're Called Vice-Principals

The vice-principal got up in front of the kids, asked them to stand, and told this assemblage of five- and six-year-olds that many of them were doomed, and not just to attend Rutgers.

"He told us to take a good look at these kids because a third of them will not graduate from high school or make it to high school because they will be too busy drugging, drinking, or getting pregnant," graduation spectator Sherri Stanard told the *Asbury Park Press*. "Whatever point he was trying to get across, he seemed to be saying these kids wouldn't make it at all."

Undoubtedly this was a matter of some confusion for the kiddies. The vice-principal asked them to stand to *illustrate* the number of kids who would drop out of high school due to drugs and pregnancy, but the five-year-old mind is not particularly keen on picking up the subtle metaphorical aspects of adult rhetoric. Heck, sometimes it has a hard time following direct declarations like "clean your room" or "stop swinging the cat." That being the case, one has to wonder how many of the kindergartners now think they *have* to drop out of school and take up drugs and sex because *that's what the vice-principal told them to do.* And you should always do what you're told.

One suspects they'll choose someone else for next year's graduation ceremony.

Sources: *Asbury Park Press*, Associated Press

* * *

"Age and wisdom don't always go together, I've found . . . Some people just become stupid with more authority."
　　　　　　　　　　　　　　　　—Terry Pratchett

CANADA, MY CANADA

Some of the notable errata from maps featured in the July 2003 edition of the semiannual magazine put out by the Canadian Tourism Commission:

- The province of Prince Edward Island is missing.
- The Yukon Territory is missing.
- Halifax, the capital city of Nova Scotia, is missing.
- The province of Newfoundland and Labrador is labeled simply "Newfoundland."
- Canada's newest territory, Nunavut, is spelled Nunavit.

You would think that the Canadian Tourism Commission would know its own country, in order to promote it effectively to others.

And to be fair, maybe it does. It simply doesn't hire people that do: the maps and and the magazine they're in, *PureCanada*, were put together by Fodor's, based in (you guessed it) the U. S. of A. The cost of the error-filled magazines, of which more than 270,000 were printed: $600,000 Canadian.

The Canadian Tourism Commission said that corrected maps will come out in their winter issue. This will be an immense relief to the citizens of Prince Edward Island and Yukon, who will finally be able to return to their homes.

Source: CBC News

A CAPITOL PERFORMANCE

He was an unconventional visual artist, and a pretty successful one as these things go. "Ray" had even won several grants and fellowships for his art and had done an artist-in-residence stint at the University of Michigan's School of Art and Design. In March 2003, Ray and his girlfriend "Mana" were traveling across the U.S., selling their artwork, and every once in a while doing little performance art pieces that they felt reflected something about the local culture. While they were in Miami, for example, Ray dressed up like a palm tree. So as Ray and Mana drove into Washington, D.C., they asked themselves: what represents this city most?

As it happens, this was right around the time the U.S. government was advising Americans to create "emergency preparedness kits" just in case the terrorists came to their hometown. One of the primary ingredients of those kits was duct tape. So Ray and Mana made themselves interesting little costumes in which they used duct tape to affix a number of objects to their bodies, like little sculptures and jars. Then, with their festive costumes, they went inside the U.S. Capitol building and commenced to dance and chant.

De-Duct-ive Reasoning

They were terribly shocked when the Capitol Police descended upon them, handcuffed them, evacuated parts of the Capitol, and then sent them to the pokey. It appears that when the Capitol Police see a couple of people with objects strapped to their body with duct tape, the first thought that comes to their minds is not "amusing performance artists exercising their First Amendment rights," but "terrorists packing heat, here to blow up the nation's seat of power." They acted accordingly.

Ray and Mana spent five days in jail. While all of the objects they had taped to themselves were later shown to be of the nonexploding variety, the two were still charged with "interstate transportation of an explosive device," a charge that apparently can be used against people the government believes were perpetrating a hoax—no actual explosive device is required.

We'd like to suggest that if you don't know that duct taping objects to your body at the nation's Capitol Building is a spectacularly dumb idea these days, you may just not be thinking hard enough.

Sources: *Washington Post*, Associated Press

* * *

"People demand freedom of speech to make up for the freedom of thought which they avoid."

—**Søren Kierkegaard**

"Today's public figures can no longer write their own speeches or books, and there is some evidence that they can't read them either."

—**Gore Vidal**

"Many wise words are spoken in jest, but they don't compare with the number of stupid words spoken in earnest."

—**Sam Levenson**

TRAIN WRECK TV

M any of the guests on Jerry Springer's talk show are not, shall we say, swinging from the highest branch of the intellectual tree. Having noted that, there are still certain examples of extreme imbecility springing from *Springer* that deserve to be noted, and we have two of them for you.

Our first shining example of Springer-osity is Paul Alexander of Wildwood, New Jersey. Mr. Alexander was a featured guest on a October 2002 episode, in which he admitted that he was engaged to the mother of the mother of his child. During the course of the show, 29-year-old Alexander noted that he had a 7-year-old child with his fiancée's daughter, Rita Koelle, age 22. Do the math there.

The Cape May County prosecutors did the math too, which is why after the show aired, they had Alexander picked up and charged with endangering the welfare of a child and second-degree sexual assault. In July 2003, Alexander was sentenced to one year in prison for criminal sexual contact. Koelle and her mother (Alexander's fiancée, remember) didn't want Alexander punted into the pokey, but as Judge Carmen Alvarez noted, "Once a person goes on national television and acknowledges committing a crime, I can't imagine a state—any state—standing idly by."

Alexander's fiancée intends to visit Alexander in the slammer. "I don't care what people think. There are stranger things than this out there," she said. (If there are, we should all run screaming into the night.)

But Wait, There's More!

Alexander may not have been aware he was admitting
to a crime when he was dazzled by the idea of being on
TV, but when Barbara Payne of Florida decided she
wanted to be on the show (on which she appeared
with her boyfriend and twin sister for an episode called
"Sneaky Sex Affairs"—her boyfriend and her twin were
supposed to be having an affair), she was aware that
she might be committing a crime by doing it. Payne, as
it happens, was under house arrest for felony burglary
and grand theft charges. When you're under house
arrest, you're not supposed to leave your house, even
when Jerry's calling.

But Payne really wanted to be on TV, so she con-
cocted a ruse that should be familiar to any college student who had a 10-page paper due and had ingested six
more beers than absolutely necessary: she sent her probation officer a fake letter from a Chicago funeral
home asserting that her grandmother had passed away,
and asked to be able to attend the funeral. The probation office denied the request, but Payne went anyway.
When her probation officer came around, Payne's
neighbors cheerfully volunteered that Payne had been
all excited about going off to be on *Springer*.

Next on Springer: "I'm in Trouble with the Law for Being on *Springer!*"

Payne was looking at a year in the slammer for her
little transgression, but Circuit Judge Thomas Gallen
took pity on her because she was seven months pregnant at the sentencing. So it's another year of probation for her. "If she hadn't been pregnant, she's looking

at a year in jail just for being stupid," said the state's prosecutor.

The worst part: Payne admitted that her boyfriend and her twin sister weren't having an affair. They all just wanted to be on TV. Man, if you can't trust what you see on *Jerry Springer*, what can you trust?

Sources: NBC10.com, Associated Press

* * *

FIRE! AND NOW A COMMERCIAL!
From the hours of 3 a.m. to 6 a.m., German television network Super RTL plays an image of a burning log, because, well, why not? It's better than infomercials, at least. However, the pixellated pyre was a little too real for one German woman in October 2003; upon waking up, she thought her television was in flames and called the local fire department. The firemen rushed over and heroically put out the fire—with the remote control. God bless 'em.

Source: Reuters

* * *

"I'd give Charles Darwin videotapes of *Geraldo*, *Beavis and Butt-head*, and *The McLaughlin Group*. I would be interested in seeing if he still believes in evolution."
                                        —Dean Koontz

NEXT TIME, HE SHOULD GO FOR A LITTLE SEQUINED NUMBER

August in northern Sweden can get a little hot—if you consider 77 degrees Fahrenheit hot. While that's what passes for cardigan weather in Phoenix, Arizona, back in the Swedish town of Umeå, bus driver Mats Lundgren felt that it was warm enough to ditch his long pants while he drove around town. No—Lundgren wasn't planning to motor about nude from the waist down, he just thought it'd be nice to wear shorts for a change.

So he went to the bus company and asked if he could wear shorts. But, no, shorts were against the company dress code. A dumb regulation, but what can you do? Everyone knows that outside of a few laws of physics and the "five second" rule about dropping food on the floor, internal company regulations are the most inflexible laws there are.

Skirting the Issue

So Lundgren did what any reasonable person would do when confronted with an inflexible yet asinine company policy: he went around it, and he showed up for work in a skirt. And a *lovely* skirt it was, too: a snappy navy blue number that showed off Lundgren's Scandinavian knees while he drove. While there was a company regulation against people wearing shorts, there was nothing about people wearing skirts. And as everyone knows, if there's no rule, then you're cool.

As a bonus, Lundgren apparently digs his new

attire. He told the *Vaesterbottens Folkblad* newspaper, "It's even better than shorts. It's unbearable driving a bus in long trousers when the sun is blazing through the windscreen, but with the skirt it feels just great."

Bet his bosses are wishing they'd let him wear shorts.

Sources: *Vaesterbottens Folkblad*, Agence France-Presse

* * *

THE IMPORTANCE OF PACING ONESELF

The Czech bus driver was having difficulty controlling his bus after he clocked in for work one morning. When he was stopped by police, he explained why: he'd been out drinking with his pals until 4 a.m. Alas, his work shift began at 4:10 a.m.

A subsequent blood test showed the bus driver had enough alcohol in him to suggest that he'd imbibed several pints of lager and a few hard liquor shots thrown in to make things interesting. Well, he probably won't have to worry about his work interfering with his drinking anymore.

Source: Reuters

#1 AT WIMBLEDON

Australians have the reputation of being the party animals of the English-speaking world, which is impressive considering that they're up against both the Americans (who invented the fraternity kegger) and the Irish (who if they didn't invent drinking, surely raised it into an art). But then, neither an Irish nor an American citizen decided to relieve himself in the center court of Wimbledon before the 2003 men's final between Roger Federer and Mark Philippoussis. It took an Aussie to do that. Three of them, actually.

A Wimbledon security guard told the British newspaper *Daily Star* that he saw the Aussies climb over the fence of the court early one Sunday morning, amble on over to the center court, and water the grass. "We heard they had climbed in and went looking for them. We found them pissing on the baseline and by the net," the security officer reported to the newspaper.

The security guard claimed that the groundskeepers knew about the incident but did nothing to clean up the mess, noting that there was no reason to bother since there was no Brit in the final match.

We should note that this report varies from the official police report, which says there were two Aussies, not three, that they didn't actually make it onto the court, and that there was "no evidence of any offense being committed." We smell a cover-up. Or, at least, that's what we hope we're smelling.

Sources: *Daily Star*, Australian Associated Press

TIPS FOR STUPID CRIMINALS

Because when smart criminals need tips,
we're all in trouble.

"HI, I'M HERE TO FIX YOUR . . ."
Today's tip: When you decide to reembark on a life of
crime, don't leave your ID at the scene.

We don't know for sure, but we expect that
"Joaquin" did not spend his free time in
California's Folsom Prison in job-training
courses. This might explain why, nine days after being
released, Joaquin was lurking around homes in Los
Angeles, searching for that certain special domicile to
break into.

Eventually Joaquin found one that appeared just
right, so, like an older, scruffier, more Y-chromosome-
laden Goldilocks, he just wandered right in through
the back door. Whereupon he found the homeowner,
who just happened to be home on that day. This particular homeowner, incidentally, happened to be Rocky
Delgadillo, City Attorney for Los Angeles. In the
entire city of L.A., there may be worse houses to break
and enter into, but off the top of our heads we can't
think of any.

So there they are, the just-released inmate and the
guy who represents the second largest city in the
United States in court (although Joaquin, who is proving himself to be kind of an "always the last to know"
sort of guy, is not up on this little fact). But Joaquin is
not entirely without guile, and suggests to Delgadillo

that he's part of a work crew at the address. But Delgadillo, being the homeowner, would probably know if he was expecting people to work at the house today, so he decides to call 911. Joaquin runs away, but leaves a backpack with identifying information. Soon enough, the LAPD hustles him off and holds him without bail.

Source: Associated Press

* * *

LAST ROUND, FELLAS

A Brazilian prison guard was feeling a bit parched after his shift and headed to a bar near the prison, where he was surprised to find three prison inmates enjoying a brew. A jailbreak? Not really.

"I told them they were arrested again and they didn't react," the guard told a local newspaper. "They even told me they were not running away, they were only having a beer." The bartender noted that they were regular patrons. They were made to go back to jail anyway.

Source: Ananova

THE REALLY STUPID QUIZ: ARTSY-FARTSY

Time for another Really Stupid Quiz! Pick the one that's true. It's not as easy as you might think (proving that the world really is a scary place to live).

1. Officers from Saudi Arabia's Committee for the Promotion of Virtue and the Prevention of Vice closed down a Medina children's theater production of skits inspired by children's tales after deciding that the story "The Three Little Pigs" was morally questionable because the pigs emerge victorious. The Koran forbids the eating of pork (Surat-ul Baqara [2]:173); many Muslims view pigs as unclean. (This is not the first time Saudi Arabia has banned depictions of pigs: the country famously banned *The Muppet Show* because of the positive portrayal of pigs by way of Miss Piggy.) The Medina show was allowed to continue after the "Pigs" segment was axed.

2. Some attendees at Edinburgh's Festival Fringe got a little more than they bargained for when they nibbled on the performers of "Edible You," an experimental participatory play in which the actors, dressed in edible costumes, would occasionally wade into the audience and encourage people to take a bite. "One of the costumes featured cold cuts and we believe that too much time under the stage lights turned the meats," noted a Festival Fringe spokesperson. As a result, two members of the "Edible You" audience took a trip to

the hospital after the performance, where they were diagnosed with mild food poisoning. The play skipped one performance but was allowed to resume after the producers promised not to let the audience eat from the cold-cut costume again.

3. A São Paulo resident sued a Brazilian television station for trauma after she inadvertently drove into a reenactment of a crime being filmed for a show. The woman was driving down a São Paulo street when she saw two armed men on motorcycles appear to take a pedestrian hostage. The woman panicked and crashed her car into a nearby truck as she tried to hightail it out of the area. "We live in a violent country, you know," she told a local newspaper. "What was I to think? There was no sign whatsoever this was a filming." The television station has agreed to compensate the twitchy driver. We're assuming a walk-on role on a show is not in the cards.

Which one is really stupid?

Answer page 311.

Source: Ananova

* * *

"There is one quality greater than hardness of heart, and that is softness of head."

—**Theodore Roosevelt**

YOU CAN BUY
BULLETS IN THE GIFT SHOP

Dandong, located in northern China, is a city of 2.3 million within the Liaodong Peninsula Economic Opening-up Zone. It's rich in all sorts of resources including tobacco, ginseng, and Chinese chestnut, as well as minerals like copper, gold, magnesium, and boron (94 percent of national reserves). It's also famed for its marble, which the locals claim is called "Champion of Marbles" by the Southeast Asian countries. To top it all off, it's home to Mianjiang Mountain Park, a nature park where, until recently, you could shoot the animals for fun.

The park was looking for an idea that would bring in more tourists when someone realized, hey, people like animals in zoos. And people like shooting things. What if we just combine the two concepts and let people shoot animals in zoos!

Let's Not and Say We Did

The folks at the Mianjiang Mountain Park quickly learned that there were some notable downsides to letting zoo patrons blast the animals. First, it made the animals nervous, and not merely the ones being shot at; several species of protected animals housed near the shooting ranges became notably jumpy when the guns started blazing. Second, it seems that the kids visiting the park were upset about the idea that the cute little creatures they had just seen might be trotted out the back door and shot. Third, animal rights activists were wound up. The park officials countered complaints by pointing out that they were only letting people shoot domesticated farmyard animals; it's not like they were shooting panda cubs or anything.

Nevertheless, stung by the bad publicity, the Mianjiang Mountain Park has phased out the shooting of zoo animals. Now you'll have to kill off the zoo animals the old-fashioned way: by throwing them high-fat snack foods that could lead to heart disease. Zoo officials would probably tell you that's just cruel.

Sources: News.com.au, Ananova, *Liaoshen Evening News*

* * *

WOOF!

A police suspect in Hamilton County, Tennessee, gave himself up when the police who were chasing him threatened to send police dogs after him—and even barked like dogs to convince the suspect that the animals were already on the scene. The suspect, who had fled police on foot after they had pulled him over for a broken taillight, was later charged with driving under the influence, driving on a revoked license, evading arrest, and a taillight violation. When told of the police's tactic to get the suspect to surrender, the judge in the case said, "I suppose as long as the officers have had their shots and don't bite, I'll allow them to continue that technique."

Source: Associated Press

DON'T DRIVE ANGRY. DON'T CRASH ANGRY, EITHER.

As our story unfolds, "Eddie," of Fond du Lac, Wisconsin, is having a few relationship issues with Mrs. Eddie, who no longer lives with him. This particular day, Eddie decides, for reasons the police later suspect have something to do with alcohol, that what he really wants to do is get into his van, drive down to his wife's home, and, oh, ram his van into her car 20 or 30 times. Just for kicks. So he gets into his van, drives to his wife's house, spots her car outside of the house, and allegedly proceeds a-rammin'. Again and again. Eddie is just a rammin' fool.

Eventually the police arrive, and they ask Eddie what in tarnation he's up to, and he tells the cops about his intense desire to reduce his wife's automobile into a compact box of ruined metal. Whereupon the cops tell him something: that's not his wife's car. Heck, the car's not even parked in front of his wife's house. As Fond du Lac officer Greg Dieke noted, "He was at the wrong house. His wife lives next door."

The cops would have taken Eddie in anyway, but now Eddie doesn't even get the satisfaction of knowing he's trashed his wife's car. He's just an angry guy with a messed-up van and bad vehicular aim. So much for good clean satisfaction.

We're guessing reconcilement isn't in the cards for this couple.

Source: Associated Press

TIPS FOR STUPID CRIMINALS

They won't make the criminals any less stupid. But they might keep them from making their stupidity known to others.

A BAD DISGUISE
Today's tip: Don't pretend to be a cop in front
of real cops. They know the difference.

For example, an off-duty Kansas City, Kansas, police officer became suspicious when a blue Ford Crown Victoria, similar to the ones used by police, tried to pull him over in June of 2003. The car had blue lights, whereas the real cop cars had red lights, too. Soon the fake cop car was being chased by a real cop car—you know, one with blue *and* red lights—which pursued the impostor car for six miles before some other real cops blew out its tires with "stop sticks." The fake cop crashed his car and then tried to escape on foot, but that chase didn't take six miles to end.

The fake cop then got a ride in a real police car. And we bet that's all he ever really wanted.

Source: Ananova

* * *

"The absurd is clear reason recognizing its limits."
—**Albert Camus**

HE GETS FIRST PLACE IN SOMETHING, ALL RIGHT

Before you start celebrating, make sure you won. Race car driver Bjorn Wirdheim, a member of the Arden International racing team, forgot that part when he was participating in a Formula 3000 race in Monte Carlo. He misjudged where the finish line was and as a result pulled off early to start accepting the congratulations of his teammates.

This was just the lucky break rival racer Nicolas Kiesa needed; he zoomed past the locationally challenged Wirdheim to take the checkered flag. Wirdheim had to settle for second place.

"I made a stupid mistake but I believe I am the moral winner," Wirdheim rationalized later. He was right about one of those.

Source: Ananova

* * *

"The trouble with the world is that the stupid are cocksure and the intelligent are full of doubt."
—**Bertrand Russell**

"Nine-tenths of wisdom consists in being wise in time."
—**Theodore Roosevelt**

THAT'S SOME BANK ERROR

I t all began when "Francesca" went to the Estado de Santa Catarina bank in Santa Catarina, Brazil. Francesca was getting money from her husband Alonzo's pension and as his wife, she didn't expect there would be any problem withdrawing the cash.

So, of course, there was a problem: the people at the bank told Francesca that she wasn't Alonzo's wife. And they knew that because Alonzo had a bank account with an entirely different woman, and *she* was his wife. They even showed Francesca the account on the computer screen with the name of her husband . . . and some other woman.

But, Honey . . .

Francesca marched home and confronted Alonzo about the bank account and the other woman. Alonzo naturally protested and told her that there was no "other woman," and that this was some weird error. But Francesca had seen the bank records, and to her, it probably seemed like the old Richard Pryor joke about a man getting caught with another woman and saying, "Who are you going to believe? Me or your own lying eyes?" In this case, Francesca believed her own eyes and divorced her still-protesting husband.

Don't "Honey" Me!

You'd think the moral of the story here is that if you're going to cheat on your wife, don't be so dumb as to put your mistress on your bank account. But you're wrong.

Because Alonzo *wasn't* cheating on his wife—it was the bank that had made the error. After five years fighting the case in the courts, Alonzo was finally able to get the bank to admit the error. As a consequence, the court had the bank pay Alonzo and Francesca about $16,500 in damages. So the moral actually is: when your husband pleads with you not to divorce him because the bank made a computer error, maybe you should entertain the notion that he might be telling the truth.

Does this mean Alonzo and Francesca are going to patch things up? Not necessarily; Francesca told the *Jornal Nacional* that she wasn't sure she wanted to get back together with her now-proven-innocent-but-still-ex ex-husband. As for Alonzo, he was philosophical: "The money is good, but it doesn't make up for a failed marriage, does it?"

Sources: *Jornal Nacional*, Ananova

* * *

"People are stupid; given proper motivation, almost anyone will believe almost anything. Because people are stupid, they will believe a lie because they want it to be true, or because they are afraid it might be true. People's heads are full of knowledge, facts, and beliefs, and most of it is false, yet they think it all true. People are stupid; they can only rarely tell the difference between a lie and the truth, and yet they are confident they can, and so are all the easier to fool."

—**Terry Goodkind**

DUMB MOVIE FESTIVAL: *THE LEAGUE OF EXTRAORDINARY GENTLEMEN* (2003)

Our Entry: *The League of Extraordinary Gentlemen*, starring Sean Connery and no one else you might know off-hand.

The Plot (Such As It Is): Nineteenth-century British adventurer and public domain action figure Allan Quatermain assembles other public domain action figures such as Captain Nemo and Tom Sawyer to keep World War I from starting 15 years or so ahead of schedule. Action scenes include a car chase in Venice, Italy (notable for having water-filled canals rather than roads), and a fisticuffs festival in which Connery, at 72, handily dispatches multiple bad guys through physical exertion without having a heart attack. Interestingly, it is based loosely on a graphic novel by Alan Moore, which is substantially smarter and more in tune with its characters.

Fun Fact: Director Stephen Norrington had such an awful time with this film (and with star Connery) that after its completion he announced his retirement from directing Hollywood films. Asked by reporters about Norrington, Connery is said to have replied, "Ask me about someone I like."

Total North American Box Office (as of 7/28/2003): $53,629,000 (source: The-Numbers.com). It has little chance of returning the estimated budget of $140 million.

The Critics Rave!

"I don't really mind the movie's lack of believability . . . What I do mind is that the movie plays like a big wind came along and blew away the script and they ran down the street after it and grabbed a few pages and shot those."—*Chicago Sun-Times*

"Your adolescent son will think it's all the dopest thing he has seen in, oh, weeks . . . Anyone without braces, however, may detect a low rumbling in the background. It's not the screws of the Nautilus you hear, but the combined sounds of Verne, H. G. Wells, Bram Stoker, Mark Twain, Oscar Wilde, Robert Louis Stevenson, and H. Rider Haggard twirling rapidly in their graves."—*Boston Globe*

"These guys have dumbed down a comic book."
—*Los Angeles Times*

"All the characters try to out-cool each other, and each spits out the most ruthlessly stupid dialogue in ages. It actually sounds like little kids playing with plastic action figures—'The enemy is mine!! Ha ha!'"—*San Francisco Examiner*

"In a way, *LXG* is extraordinary. Despite Connery and Moore's source material, it's an extraordinary waste of time and an astounding piece of incoherent storytelling. The combination of intricate, dazzling designs and absurd violence is almost unique. I've certainly never seen anything like it—and I hope I never do again."—*Chicago Tribune*

"I found myself in the League of I Want Out of Here."
—*Reel Talk*

NOT VERY COOL

You think it's hot where you are. Try being an allied soldier in Iraq in the summer. Not only is it blistering hot—and no, it doesn't help that it's a dry heat—but as a soldier your discomfort is compounded by the fact you're wearing a bunch of heavy equipment and weaponry. Fact is, if you aren't sweating like a pig, it's because you probably already had sunstroke.

Cooling-off Period
It was under these conditions that a lance corporal with the British contingent, came up with what he thought was a very cool idea. It's hot out here in the sun, he reasoned. But inside this conveniently placed walk-in refrigeration unit, it's refreshingly cool! I'll just wander inside and have a quick nap. And that's what he did—and that's where he was found by his fellow soldiers some undetermined time later, in an alarming stage of hypothermia. His pals hustled him off to the medics; he suffered minor injuries but major embarrassment and initially tried to suggest that he had somehow managed to get accidentally locked in.

No one was buying, but everyone understood. "The lad was a bit of a fool to think he could have a kip in a fridge and not suffer from pretty bad consequences," said a British soldier. "But it's so hot here that most people kind of understand what was behind his bizarre logic."

It was probably a dry cool.

Source: ABC News Online (Australia)

THAT'S WHAT YOU GET FOR CUTTING IN LINE

From the lunch line in kindergarten on you've been told: *don't cut in line.* Cutting in line is rude; more than that, it's elitist. What you're saying when you cut in line is that you're better than the people who are patiently waiting their turn. Egalitarians that we are, we hate that. Which is why, in the grand list of People to Be Punished, line-cutters are right at the top with telemarketers and people who use cell phones at movies. So this tale of line-cutting karmic revenge should satisfy you.

"Arnold" was in Albany, waiting for a bus to take him to New York City. When it arrived, Arnold didn't see the point in waiting in line to board with the rest of the rabble. So he just cut ahead, hopped on the bus, and took a seat. This flagrant disregard of the other passengers incensed the bus driver, who told the cops. The cops arrived and asked Arnold for his ticket. Arnold reached into his pocket and pulled it out, but as he was doing so, a little extra something fell out of his pocket: a joint.

The cops wanted to take Arnold to jail. Arnold attempted a physical protest. It didn't work. While at the sheriff's lockup, Arnold showed he was a man of surprises, since in addition to the aforementioned pot, he was also carrying 18 small plastic bags of crack cocaine. These, it should be noted, weren't exactly in his pocket—he had secreted them somewhere else. No wonder he was in a rush to get back to New York City.

Arnold was charged with unlawful possession of marijuana, resisting arrest, felony counts of tampering with evidence, and drug possession. His next bus trip may be to prison. Wonder if he'll try to cut in line for *that* bus.

Source: Associated Press

* * *

DO YOU SMELL THAT?

Let's suppose you've got 170 pounds of marijuana in your apartment, which you then decide to dry out by cranking up your thermostat to 100 degrees. How many air fresheners do you need to hide the massive pot funk emanating from your residence?

Well, it'll need to be more than the single, lone Glade air freshener five Chicago college students put near their front door. The poor household product was simply overwhelmed by the drugs, which was probably why the neighbors complained and the cops came around. "Once you got off the elevator you could smell it," one cop said. Our students were arrested and the pot (worth an estimated $467,000) hauled away. The air freshener, we assume, stayed.

Source: *Chicago Sun-Times*

ULTIMATE MELLOW HARSHER

The old adage says that time heals all wounds. Likewise, science tells us that people who smoke a lot of pot damage their memory, at least temporarily. Put the two together, and you may end up with a couple like "Gio" and "Gia," from the Liguria region of Italy. This older couple (he 66, she 57) needed someplace to grow their marijuana plants. Someplace far from the prying eyes of the authorities. Someplace quiet and out of the way, where their plants wouldn't be bothered. Say, at the grave site of their son.

Two things here. First, man, that's just so *not* cool. How far do those plant roots reach down? Where are those soil nutrients coming from? Here's a hint: they're in a cemetery. By the grave of this couple's *son*. Did they ever stop to consider that before they toked up? Second, of course, no matter where you put six-foot-high cannabis plants, sooner or later someone's bound to notice, especially if you put them in a public area, like a graveyard.

And so the authorities did notice, and, perhaps tipped off by the name on the headstone by which all the pot plants were congregating, paid a visit to Gio and Gia, who readily admitted to "using the cemetery for illegal acts." Police also found pot plants in Gio and Gia's courtyard, where presumably nothing besides the occasional pet might be buried.

Perhaps from here on out, Gio and Gia will just leave flowers. Let's hope they're not poppies.

Source: Ananova

NOT THE RECORD TO HOLD IF YOU WANT TO MEET GROOVY CHICKS

R adhakant Bajpai has hair. Award-winning hair. Long, flowing hair of the sort that people can't help but notice—indeed, hair that cries out for attention. And attention it has received, including the attention of the *Guinness Book of World Records*. This repository of all things world-record-y has declared that Radhakant has the longest hair in the world.

What's so dumb about that, you ask? This: it's his ear hair, people.

Yes, Mr. Bajpai of India has tufts of hair sprouting out of his ears to the length of over five inches. That's more than half an inch longer than the tufts of the previous record holder Anthony Victor, also of India—and *that's* a fact that should have the UN scrambling to send emergency stores of personal grooming kits to the subcontinent as quickly as possible. Mr. Bajpai proclaims that he was inspired in his strange and inexplicable quest for auditory hirsuteness by former ear-hair record holder B.D. Tyagi, of Bhopal, India.

What Is Going On Down There?

Although most men in the world would rather die than have ear hair long enough to braid—and rightly so— Bajpai is reveling in his disturbing, newfound fame. "Making it to the Guinness records is indeed a special occasion for me and my family. God has been very kind to me," he said to the *Hindustan Times*. Which makes you wonder about his standards for divine kindness.

So, guys, the next time you're yanking out those unsightly ear hairs, just remember that you're blowing your chance for being in the *Guinness Book of World Records*. Good for you!

Sources: *Hindustan Times*, Ananova

* * *

WHY YOU DON'T CHEW ON HAIR

Surgeons in India removed a pound of hair from the stomach of a 24-year-old woman who suffered from trichophagia, a psychological disorder that compels one to ingest hair, which is indigestible and can collect in the stomach. The freaky wrinkle: it wasn't her hair, it was her mother's. The family of the woman admitted she had this thing for eating her mother's hair, but they refused to provide information on how she obtained the hair.

Source: *Chandigarh Tribune*

YOU CAN PUT
THEM RIGHT NEXT TO
YOUR FAKE CREDIT CARDS

Worried that your pathetic attempts to attract hot dates are not nearly pathetic enough? We've got the thing for you: fake ATM slips.

The idea is simplicity itself: the fake ATM slip has both a fake bank (Fidelity National Bank & Savings), a fake withdrawal amount ($400), and most importantly, a fake remaining balance—$314,159.26. The idea is that the person you're trying to impress will take your phone number just to get you out of their hair, then you jot down your number on one of these fake ATM slips and scoot it over. Your intended target will be so overwhelmed by the numbers on the ATM slip that he or she will be willing to set aside any previous objections in order for the chance to mine your savings account like the gold diggers of old. And who wouldn't want that?

All That Glitters, Baby

There are drawbacks, of course. Most obviously, the whole reason you're using the fake ATM slip is because you *don't* have $314,159.26 in your bank account, and sooner or later the object of your affections will figure that out, probably after that third date at a restaurant where paper napkins are only grudgingly supplied. Ultimately, no matter how desperate you are for companionship, it isn't easy spending time with someone who basically sees you as a cash register with a pulse.

Finally, on the extremely off chance that the person you've enticed with a fake ATM slip actually does turn out to be a wonderful human being who you could spend the rest of eternity with, you're totally hosed because your very first contact with him or her was a total lie. And it's just hard to come back from that sort of betrayal.

Sure, in movies, people who pull stunts like this are forgiven and live happily ever after. But if you were in the movies, you wouldn't have needed the fake ATM slip to begin with. It's a vicious cycle.

Forget the fake ATM slips. Be honest. At least that way, when your first dinner date is cafeteria-style, your date will know that it really is the best that you can do.

Source: *Charlotte Observer*

* * *

"Genius may have its limitations, but stupidity is not thus handicapped."

—Elbert Hubbard

"You can swim all day in the Sea of Knowledge and still come out completely dry. Most people do."

—Norman Juster

"Every man has his follies—and often they are the most interesting thing he has got."

—Josh Billings

FIRST WE TAKE AUSTRIA, THEN LIECHTENSTEIN WILL FALL LIKE A PLUMP GRAPE

Austria is famed for being the birthplace of Arnold Schwarzenegger and for having something to do with that Amadeus guy in that movie our music teacher made us watch.

But for all its obvious contributions to the world's critically short supply of Teutonically inflected one liners, it's not a country that anyone realistically imagines to be near the top of the list for potential invasion by enemy forces. Yes, sure, the Russians *did* go through Vienna at the end of WWII, and the entire country was occupied for 10 years by the Allied powers. But that was years ago. Today, Austria can be largely assumed safe from invasion.

An Army of One

However, as Thomas Jefferson once said, "The price of liberty is eternal vigilance." That's why when, in May 2003, "Hans," a 53-year-old Austrian forester, spotted someone tromping through the woods wearing camouflage and sporting what appeared to be a rifle, he assumed the worst: invaders, perhaps indirectly blaming Austria for unleashing *Last Action Hero* on an unsuspecting globe. Hans didn't wait to see the whites of their eyes; he called the local police, who in turn helped to initiate a major military alert. In no time the woods were crawling with dogs and specially trained "Cobra" combat forces; helicopters scanned the invasion area from above. The Austrian navy, still reeling from the defection of Captain Von Trapp, could only look on nervously.

Eventually the invading "army" was discovered. It consisted of a 15-year-old boy dressed in camo, carrying a wooden toy gun. He was on his way to a friend's house and used the woods as a shortcut. The boy said that all the months of watching the fighting in Iraq had made him want to go out and play soldiers.

Tonight, Austria sleeps, safe from invasion. Hans, back in the forest, will receive ribbing about the incident from friends and woodland animals alike for the rest of his life. And the world remains unavenged for *Last Action Hero*.

* * *

SEMPER FINANCE

Just because the U.S. Marine Corps gives you a credit card doesn't mean you can use it for whatever you want. This was discovered by a Marine staff sergeant who was sentenced to 14 months in a military prison for making some interesting unauthorized purchases on a Corps credit card. Some of the purchases: a car, a motorcycle, and a boob job. All told she made $129,709 in improper purchases. In addition to jail time, she was demoted, discharged, and fined. No word if she has to give back her purchases, even the implantable ones.

Source: Associated Press

HISTORICAL DUMBOSITY: BAD FOOD IDEAS

The average grocery store in the United States and Canada holds thousands and thousands of product lines, and every one of them is a winner—in that they've managed to get on the shelves and stay there. But for every success story like Twinkies or Orville Redenbacher, there's about a hundred culinary missteps that hit the shelves for a little while before being relegated to oblivion. Here are some of those sad, wan bad food ideas.

Wine & Dine Dinners: These boxed dinners, created by wine distributor Heublein in the 1970s, were pasta dishes with sauce and a little bottle of cooking wine to use as you cooked the foods. But you know how people love not to read directions. Most people who bought the stuff thought you were supposed to drink the wine, and as anyone who's ever sampled cooking wine knows, it's not really for drinking. This is one of those "got bought once" things.

Gerber's Singles: In 1974 the famed baby food company thought: hey, why not make food for people with teeth? And so it came out with a whole line of foods for grown-ups, in convenient single-serving form. And they put it in the same jars into which they put their baby food. Somehow, single grown-ups just couldn't hang with the idea of eating their food out of a jar that resembled what strained peas came out of when they

y motor control. The Singles disappeared
ter.

Jell-O for Salads: Watch it wiggle, see it jiggle, cool
and . . . vegetable-y? Yes, that's right, the folks at Jell-O
thought that the American consumer might go for
Jell-O in flavors like tomato and celery. But the
99.98% of Americans who would rather saw off an arm
than ask for the recipe for Tomato Aspic Salad (2
packages sugar-free lemon Jell-O, 1 cup boiling water,
2 small cans tomato sauce, 1 tablespoon Worcestershire
sauce, 1 teaspoon lemon juice—mix well and run
screaming from this unholy culinary monstrosity)
decided not to go there.

Reddi Bacon: What could be more of a natural comple-
ment to a whipped dessert topping than foil-wrapped
bacon you place in your toaster? That was the thinking
at the Reddi-Wip company, which suggests someone
over at Reddi R&D spent a little too much time huffing
the aerosol out of those whipped topping cans. Reddi
Bacon failed because people just didn't make the natural association between dessert topping and breakfast
meat, and there was also the minor problem that when
you put fat-laden meat into a toaster, foil-wrapped or
not, it has a tendency to leak hot fat, which then has a
tendency to catch fire. An exciting time at breakfast, to
be sure. But that's not what everyone wants.

Campbell's No-Salt Soups: The soup giant put out
soups with no salt in them, leading the American public to realize that soup without salt needs a little some-

thing extra to make it palatable. Like, oh, we don't know, maybe salt. There was also the fact that Campbell's ditched its familiar red-and-white can design for a bright blue-and-white color scheme, which was also off-putting to consumers. To quote Steinberg: "The result looked unnatural, almost terrifying—the sort of thing Campbell's would use to package a line of radioactive soups: 'Plutonium and Stars,' 'Cream of Deuterium,' 'Heavy Broth.'" Mmm, mmm, good!

(The examples here are culled Neil Steinberg's classic on bad ideas: *Complete & Utter Failure: A Celebration of Also-Rans, Runners-Up, Never-Weres and Total Flops.* If you don't own this book, you should.)

* * *

AN EXPANDING MARKET

North Americans are getting larger—and manufacturers of home scales are answering their increasing needs. The Canadian Broadcasting Corporation reported that scale makers in the United States are raising the top weight on their scales. Scales, which once ranged from 270 to 300 pounds, will now range from 300 to 400 pounds. "Four hundred seemed a reasonable number. If we find consumers need a higher capacity, we have the technology to do it," said Jennifer Hansard, marketing director for scale maker Health-O-Meter.

Source: CBC.ca

THE 411 ON 911

Contrary to the view held by the classic rap group Public Enemy, most of the time calling 911 is not a joke—it's a good number to call in an emergency.

"Harvey," a 22-year-old resident of West Palm Beach, Florida, decided that 911 also had another function: personal entertainment. So he called. And he called. And he called. All told, in the space of two months in 2003, he called 911 *nine hundred times*—200 times on June 23 alone.

And what would he say when he called? Well, sometimes he'd say a cop had been shot. Sometimes he'd say he wanted to shoot a cop. And sometimes, when he couldn't think of anything to say, he'd just hoot into the 911 operator's ear like an animal. You would think that after the first hundred or so calls, the 911 folks would catch on and ignore him. But it's not like that. Unlike in the famous story of the boy who cried wolf, every 911 call has to be checked out. So every phone call Harvey made took resources away from the people who really were having heart attacks, battling kitchen fires, or being devoured by wolves.

Maybe Jimmy Is a Big White Rabbit

So it was only a matter of time before the police descended upon Harvey and nabbed him for unlawful use of the 911 system (a misdemeanor). Harvey claimed that his "friend" Jimmy was the one making the phone calls and that he'd give Jimmy a good talking to. But when the calls didn't stop, the cops went back to Harvey, and an investigation uncovered that "Jimmy" was the name of Harvey's parrot. Admittedly, this would explain the animal sounds. Nevertheless, it appears that the police believe it was the guy with the opposable thumbs who was making the calls.

So heed Harvey's lesson: play with 911, and the cops will show up, all right. They just won't be there to *help* you.

Source: Associated Press

* * *

CRISPY CASH

The guy who robbed the Perkins Family Restaurant in North Charleston, South Carolina, was smart enough to bring a blowtorch to cut a hole in the restaurant's safe. But he wasn't smart enough not to let the blowtorch set fire to the money inside the safe. Surveillance tapes show the burglar, wearing a T-shirt over his head to hide his identity, rushing to the kitchen sink to get water to put out the flaming cash. Three thousand dollars was stolen, most of it, police suspected, at least partially burned, which would make it difficult to spend. All that heroic effort for nothing.

Source: Charleston *Post and Courier*

DUBIOUS DECOR AWARD

Since September 11, 2001, airports everywhere have been answering the call for better security by adding new scanning measures for luggage, being more vigilant about the identities of passengers, and buying fake plants.

What? You're not exactly sure how the purchase of fake plants aids in the global struggle against terrorism? Well then clearly you're not a member of the Airport Authority of India (AAI), which in May 2003 allocated roughly $2.7 million to replace the live plants at India's many airports with more than 22,000 fake ones.

The thinking was that live plants need to be watered, which means extra staff trolling about the airport—extra staff that could be infiltrated by terrorists. Eliminate the live plants and you eliminate gardeners wandering around, and that's one less possible point of entry for the terrorists. But you have to have *some* sort of greenery—otherwise the airports would just look industrial and creepy. Fake plastic trees solve the problem.

Voodoo Economics
The thing is, the Airport Authority of India didn't have $2.7 million just lying around to buy fake plants. (Who does?) So its members came up with some real out-of-the-box thinking: why not take the money that had been allocated for boundary walls and fire safety and buy fake plants with that? Because, you know, the terrorists wouldn't just try to sneak into the airport over the fences. That'd be too obvious. And once

you've eliminated the "terrorist gardener" scenario, you've also apparently eliminated much of your need for fire safety.

The AAI's potted-plant decision was such creative thinking that when the *Indian Express* newspaper asked India's federal civil aviation minister Syed Shahnawaz Hussain about it, he was taken entirely by surprise. Hussain promised to investigate immediately. In the meantime, enjoy your flight to the subcontinent! And especially enjoy those fake plants.

Source: Ananova

* * *

WHERE WAS SMOKEY THE BEAR WHEN WE NEEDED HIM?

Cigarettes start forest fires, and of all people, we expect a fireman to know that. So it's with some measure of disappointment that we note that a fire in British Columbia was caused by a fireman improperly flicking his cigarette while installing a satellite dish in his back-yard. To the fireman's credit, as soon as he realized what he'd done, he ran to his neighbors' to warn them of the approaching wall of flame. But when you've started a large fire that causes 8,500 people to flee from their homes and destroys 65 homes, owning up to it is still a little weak. In the aftermath, the fireman wasn't sure if he should go back to the fire station: "I'm not sure if they want me to work there anymore."

Source: Canadian Press

HONESTY IS THE BEST POLICY, EXCEPT IN CIRCUMSTANCES LIKE THESE

P reface: drinking and driving—bad, bad, *bad.* Don't do it. But for the sake of argument, let's say you're pulled over by the cops for a routine traffic stop and the cop asks you if you've been drinking. *Acceptable* answers include "Of course not," "Not since that liver replacement," and, in a pinch, "You'd have to ask my lawyer."

An unacceptable answer would be what "Dieter" told the cop who pulled him over in Essen, Germany, in July 2003: "Twenty beers at most if you want me to be perfectly honest, officer. But that's it, really." In Dieter's case, this caused the officer, no doubt impressed with our man's honesty, to administer a breath test, which appeared to confirm the mighty amount of alcohol in Dieter's bloodstream. Dieter gets a lot of credit for unstinting adherence to the truth, but he also got his license revoked.

Raymund Sandach, a spokesman for Essen police, had this to say about Dieter: "I've no idea why he told them. Maybe because he was drunk."

Source: Reuters

I'D KILL FOR THIS PART!

Esteban," an actor in Colombia, *really* wanted a
part in director Emilio Marlle's new film. He was
sick of his lot in life as an actor on a Colombian
soap opera, *Milagros de Amor,* and was ready to move
up to the big time. Not satisfied with the traditional
ways of getting a role—setting up an audition, sending
a tape, showing the studio head risqué pictures—
Esteban decided to try something different. Something
daring. Something felonious.

While director Marlle was shooting another feature, Esteban walked onto the film location and, armed
with a prop gun and wearing a mask, proceeded to kid-
nap Marlle off the set of the film. Marlle found himself
being hustled toward a getaway car when Esteban
ripped off his mask, revealed himself as an actor, and
explained how much he'd really like to work with
Marlle on his next film.

Marlle didn't call Esteban's agent; he called the
cops. And then he told *UOL Tabloide* in no uncertain
terms that the two of them would be unlikely to work
together, *ever:* "That ass**** almost killed me," Marlle
said. "I have not chosen the actor for this part yet and
I hope that other actors don't follow his example."

As for Esteban, no doubt he'll be looking forward
to his next role as That Good-Looking, Dumb Actor
Guy in a Nasty Colombian Prison. It's the role of a
lifetime!

Sources: *UOL Tabloide,* Ananova

ON THE OTHER HAND, WOULD YOU WANT THIS GUY ON YOUR JURY?

J ury duty: one of your constitutional rights, sure, and juries are nice to have around if you should ever be found by the police with a suitcase of counterfeit twenties, a badger, a wad of duct tape, and no compelling explanation. Be that as it may, jury duty's also a bit of a pain. Really, if you're going to have to miss work, better you should miss it while on the beach tanning yourself into coppery lizardhood, rather than sitting in a box with 11 fellow citizens, trying to stay awake while you listen to some miscreant's lawyer try to explain how it was the *badger's* suitcase, not his client's. That's why so many of us will try to find a way to skip jury duty.

"Ted" of Alto, Michigan, was one of those people. His excuses for skipping jury duty in April 2003 were many. His car was in the shop. He had work. He had a kid to watch. But rather than offer up any of these perfectly valid excuses in the hopes of getting off the hook, Ted pursued a crafty alternate strategy: he just didn't go.

The Wheels of Justice Grind Away
Unfortunately this strategy did not dissuade the Kent County Circuit Court from its attempt to make Ted participate in a hallowed tradition. The court called Ted to find out where he might have been during those missing three days. Ted called the court back,

got the answering machine, and unleashed your basic barrage of obscenities into the machine. Ted later maintained that he was unaware his tirade was actually being recorded, perhaps assuming, and one could say not unjustifiably, that the name "answering machine" implies only that the phone is being answered. However, this still leaves open the question of what Ted was doing hollering obscenities into a phone if he thought no one was listening. Or, alternatively, if he thought he was on the phone with a live person, why yelling at them would be any better.

Not surprisingly, Ted eventually found himself at the courthouse—not to serve jury duty, but to explain to Judge Donald Johnston why he decided to shirk his obligations as a citizen. Ted quickly annoyed the judge. "Basically, he said he was too busy to be bothered with jury duty," Johnston told *Grand Rapids Press*. Judge Johnston decided Ted wasn't too busy for a trip to the stony lonesome, and sentenced the jury-ditching Ted to jail time: three days, probably not coincidentally the same number of days Ted ditched jury duty.

"I never thought I'd end up in jail," said Ted, from jail. He then blamed his stint in the big house on the judge having a bad day, and noted that he still had no intention of spending time in a jury box. He appears to have missed the irony that he was saying this from a completely different sort of box, the sort of box one usually sees only after spending time in front of a jury.

Source: Associated Press

JUST SAY NO, EXCEPT TO US

When you're a professional tennis player, there are lots of things that you're not supposed to put into your body—and the Association of Tennis Professionals (ATP) will happily test what comes *out* of your body to make sure they're not there. One of these banned substances is the anabolic steroid nandrolone. Anabolic steroids can artificially increase your muscle mass and thereby increase your performance, and for that reason they're banned.

In March 2003, Czech tennis player Bohdan Ulihrach tested positive for nandrolone, and the penalty from the ATP was swift and harsh: a two-year suspension, a fine of over $66,000, and the loss of 100 ranking points (which seems like adding insult to injury, considering he wasn't allowed to play). But that's the breaks when you do drugs.

But did he? In May, the ATP noticed that an unusually high number of urine samples from players were coming back with nandrolone in them.

Is It in You?
ATP looked into it and found the culprit: an electrolyte-replacement product given to tennis players by ATP trainers.

Or to put it more simply: the reason players were testing positive for steroids was because the ATP was giving it to them. Oh, *accidentally*, of course. Even so, this is just the sort of move that makes conspiracy theorists twitch with delight. It's also why in July 2003, new ATP guidelines forbade its trainers from handing out certain electrolyte tablets and vitamins.

As for Bohdan Ulihrach, he was reinstated and declared eligible to play. And for everyone else, the ATP said that the small amounts of nandrolone players ingested won't have long-term effects.

Source: Reuters

* * *

A BIG CROC

The University of Florida's sports teams are famously known as the "Gators"—named after the state's famous reptile inhabitant. So it was more than mildly embarrassing when the university's 2003 football guide was published with a crocodile, not an alligator, on the cover. Can't tell the two species apart? You're not alone: neither could the agency hired by the university to find a picture for the guide's cover. "We asked for an alligator, we paid for an alligator and unfortunately we did not get an alligator," said a university spokesman. Check out the Everglades, people.

Source: Associated Press

* * *

"One man alone can be pretty dumb sometimes, but for real bona fide stupidity, there ain't nothin' can beat teamwork."

—Edward Abbey

WAIT TILL YOU HEAR WHAT THEY CALL THEIR HARD LIQUOR!

You'd think that the citizens of the tiny German town of Krov would be thrilled at the prospect of a new multimillion-dollar community center opening in their town. But no— a substantial number of the town's 2,500 citizens, including the mayor, were hopping mad about it. Why? It's all in the name.

You see, Krov, which is in the Mosel region of Germany, has a popular local wine that's known as "Krover Nacktarsch." This nicely textured wine is described as "smooth and tasty" by sellers and brings the town some fame in wine circles. So the Krov city council wanted to name the new community center after the wine. Thus the name *Nacktarschhalle*.

What's the Big Deal?

Well, *Nacktarsch*, translated saucily into English, means "naked ass." This concept is cheekily illustrated by the label of the wine variety, which typically shows a wayward *kinder*, his *lederhosen* down around his chubby ankles, being spanked by his parent.

Nacktarschhalle, by extension, means "Naked Ass Hall," and that's what got Krov's mayor, the august Elmar Trossen, all riled up. "Can you imagine being invited to a wedding reception or holding a classical concert at the Naked Ass Centre?" he complained. Regardless, the Krov city council voted 11 to 4 for *Nacktarschhalle*. Naked Ass Hall it is.

So the next time you're in the Mosel region of Germany and you're invited to come on down to the Naked Ass Hall, try not to get too excited. It's not what you think.

Source: Ananova

* * *

BEWARE THE UNDERPANTS!

Flying underpants were blamed for a car crash in Germany. Apparently a van full of naked guys tossed their underwear into a passing car on the autobahn. The underwear landed on the driver's face (eeewww!), and the driver, temporarily blinded by the skivvies, proceeded to ram into a truck directly in front of him. No one was hurt, and the naked van guys got away. Police admitted they couldn't imagine why people were driving around naked on the autobahn in the first place.

Source: Reuters

* * *

"The only thing that ever consoles a man for the stupid things he does is the praise he always gives himself for doing them."

—Oscar Wilde

HANDS DOWN, THE STICKIEST TAX SITUATION YET

On the one hand, you can't blame "Clive." He was an unemployed factory worker, down on his luck, looking for the benefits he was legally owed by Britain's Inland Revenue bureau. You certainly can't say he didn't make an effort to deal with the bureau: he made more than 200 attempts to get in touch with them about his benefits, to no avail. Finally, it came to the point where he damn well needed those benefits. He had kids to feed.

However, sticking your hand to someone's desk with superglue is probably not the most effective way to make your point. This is what Clive did in May 2003. He walked into the Bridgwater, Somerset, office of Inland Revenue and talked to members of the staff there about his predicament. When they told him that they couldn't help him, Clive took his hand, slathered it with superglue, and slapped it down on a desk. Then he told the staff he'd remove it—and him-self—when he got the benefits he'd come for.

That Was Jive, Clive

Reasons why this is dumb: first and most obviously, the whole point of superglue is that it's extremely adhesive, so while slapping down the hand was quickly and easily done, getting it back up without removing large chunks of one's fingers is something of a challenge. (Clive might have then been able to claim disability, but considering why he was at the

Inland Revenue office in the first place, it's not like
he could expect the payment anytime soon.)

Second, as Clive well knew, the wheels of bureaucracy grind ever so slowly, and when one has super-
glued oneself to a desk, it's difficult to take a little
time off for a potty break.

Third, they could have just called the cops and
hauled Clive, desk and all, to the slammer.

Sticking Up for Himself

The last part, at least, Clive had prepared for. In fact,
as he told the London *Times*, he had fully intended to
get arrested. "I wanted to embarrass the Revenue and
to get them to do something for people like me," he
said. "I'm just a hardworking man who was hammered
into a corner. Sticking my hand to a table is not the
sort of thing I do for a hobby."

So overall, a dumb move. And yet, it worked.
A half hour later, Clive was unstuck and out of the
office with a check for £400. But be warned, all you
benefits seekers: this is one of those dumb moves that
probably works only once.

Sources: London *Times*, Ananova

* * *

"If you leap into a Well, Providence is not bound to
fetch you out."

—**Thomas Fuller**

DRIVEN TO DRINK

W e like efficiency, even when it comes to doing stupid things. For that reason, we'd like to present an "Efficiency in Stupidity" award to a man from Westmoreland, Tennessee, who allegedly did all these stupid things in rapid order:

1. Carrying an open container in the car. Now, we're the first to admit that an open container of alcohol doesn't *automatically* mean you're drinking when you're driving. But then again, if you're *not* drinking and driving, what are you doing with an open container in the car? Flicking the alcohol on you to keep yourself refreshingly moist? Savoring the car-filling aroma of beer? Preparing for road accidents that require the immediate topical application of Budweiser?

2. Littering. At some point during the drive, said open container was hurled—or launched itself—from the car our man was driving. Littering isn't very nice; for one thing, it makes a mess on the side of the road, which has to be cleaned up by well-meaning Adopt-a-Highway people. You may think that by littering you're giving these do-gooders something to do on Saturday afternoons, but if you didn't litter, and no one had to adopt a highway to pick up your crap, these people would find something else to do.

Also, your trash might actually hit another car, as happened with our man, whose flung beer can smacked right into the windshield of a Tennessee

Highway Patrol car. The Tennessee highway patrolman, not at all amused at having his vehicle assaulted by beer, gave chase.

3. Evading arrest. Our escapee must have been aware that the Tennessee highway patrolman wanted to talk to him, what with the flashing lights and sirens. But since he was very close to the the state line, he sped up. As he was doing this, he performed his fourth stupid act of the day.

4. Crash and carry. Sad. Our guy *did* make it across the state line into Kentucky. But if he thought he was home free, he should have guessed again. Who knows? Maybe he forgot there was a license plate on his car. Police in Kentucky, inclined to help their Tennessee brethren, tracked the license plate to a rental car company. The driver may have thought since it wasn't his car, he couldn't be tracked. But the rental car company keeps records of who it rents its cars to.

And so, the police found their way to our driver, who was charged with reckless endangerment with a deadly weapon and felony evading arrest, littering, and violation of the state's open container law. See, the police can be efficient, too.

Source: *Gallatin News Examiner*

BAD PARENTS, IN CARS

K ids, cars, and stupid parents: a bad combination. As proven by "Leon" of Tampa, Florida, who had a hankerin' to catch the pole-dancing girls over at a local strip joint. There was just one little problem. Well, actually, four little problems, aged eight, six, four, and one and a half: Leon's kids. Strip clubs are known for many things, but having on-site child care is not one of them. This presented Leon with a quandary: how to see scantily clad women with four kids in tow?

Daddy Dearest
Leon's solution: the family automobile. Leon drove the kids to the parking lot of the strip club, got out, and locked the kids in. Then he headed into the bar. A satisfactory solution for Leon, but less so for the kids; after a little while, they got antsy and the youngest started bawling. This attracted the attention of the club's security officers, who as you might imagine were a little surprised to see a car full of kids in their parking lot. They called the bar's manager. "We asked where their parents were," manager Bob Finkelsen said to a *St. Petersburg Times* reporter. "They said they didn't know."

Pin the Tale on the Daddy
Finkelsen considered making an announcement over the bar's PA, but called the cops instead. When they arrived, Leon's excuse for being in the strip bar was

that he was only using the toilet services. Nice try, except for the fact that the toilets were in the lobby, and Leon was in the bar proper. He'd even paid the $20 cover charge to get in; the lobby, we should note, was cover-charge-free. A pretty steep pee fee.

The kids, scared but unhurt, were picked up by their aunt. Leon was arrested on four counts of child endangerment and held on $30,000 bail. We're guessing that it'll be a while before he's trusted to take the kids on another field trip.

Mommy's Visit to the Slammer

Now, before you get all smug and think "Isn't that just like a man," we'd like to trot out Exhibit B in the bad-parents-with-cars sweepstakes: "Karen," from the Commonwealth of Pennsylvania. Karen's bad luck was having a husband who's locked away in one of those state prisons. So she drove to the prison with her three-year-old daughter to spend a little family time. But when she got there, her daughter wasn't on the visitors list.

At this point, it might be natural to have sympathy for Karen, who traveled all the way to the prison to see her man, just to be turned away at the door. Not so when you learn how she dealt with this little problem: she walked her toddler back to the car, opened the trunk, put her in it, closed the trunk, and went back inside the prison to visit with her hubby. We're pretty sure that's not suggested in any parenting guide on this planet.

A Shut and Open Case

Police estimate the kid was in the trunk about 40 minutes before prison guards heard her and got her out. The little girl was all right and went off with the authorities. So did Karen—but with different authorities and to a different place, namely jail, where she was charged with endangerment and attempted aggravated assault.

So, yeah, that's as bad as a carload of kids at a strip joint.

Next time, find a sitter.

Sources: *St. Petersburg Times* (Florida), Associated Press

* * *

DUBIOUS ACHIEVEMENTS IN ALCOHOL

A landscape architect in Queensland was awarded the somewhat dubious honor of being perhaps the drunkest female driver ever pulled over in Australia when her Breathalyzer reading clocked in at .401, which is more than eight times Queensland's legal limit. To put this in perspective: most people slip into a coma when their blood alcohol count is around .350 and die when it reaches .500. According to her lawyer, her excuse was that she drank four bottles of vanilla essence, which is more than 50 percent alcohol. That stuff is for baking, dearie.

Source: *Herald Sun* (Australia)

BANG! YOU'RE DUMB

They thought it would be fun. Or maybe they were just stoned. Whatever the reason, teenagers "Chet" and "Joel" took to the roads of Pittsburgh to start their shooting spree. Their ammunition: paintballs. These balls of paint are nonfatal but kind of painful (as anyone who's ever been hit with one can tell you), and of course, the paint is tough as heck to get out of your clothes. Normally, paintball-gun wielders are confined to a paintball field, usually found in a scroungy wood or a former landfill on the edge of town, where the only people who get shot are paintball enthusiasts and the occasional office work group on a dubious teamwork-building exercise. But Chet and Joel decided they needed to share the love.

And oh, the high jinks they had, driving about and pinging paintballs. Until, that is, they made their fatal error and decided to paintball the houses near the intersection of Broad and Winebiddle Streets, in the Garfield neighborhood of Pittsburgh. Our boys drove by once, letting loose a hail of paint, and had so much fun that they decided to go around for a second pass. That's when one of the residents of the area decided to wage his own battle by pumping a dozen *real* bullets into Chet and Joel's vehicle. Chet caught one of those bullets in his arm; Joel got one in the ass.

Pittsburgh police Lt. Philip Dacey noted, "It looks like they picked the wrong area."

Wait, there's more. Chet and Joel managed to drive their bullet-riddled selves to the hospital. It was there the police discovered that our bright boys, in addition to carrying gunshot wounds, were also carrying heroin and crack cocaine. So after being shot at, they were brought up on possession charges as well as a charge for allegedly having a loaded paintball gun. Now that's what you call some big fun!

Just remember that guns don't shoot morons with paintball guns. *People* shoot morons with paintball guns. And real guns, too. According to the Pittsburgh police, those people are still at large. So keep the paintball guns holstered, Hondo.

Source: WTAE-TV (Pittsburgh)

* * *

ZAP!

It's not nice to zap people with tasers, and it's especially not nice to zap homeless people with tasers. But if you're going to do something as stupidly evil as that, as four Cleveland, Ohio, teenagers thought they must in August 2003, it's not wise to record yourself doing it on videotape. Because if the videotape is in your car when it breaks down directly in front of the city's justice center, you might be arrested for assault, as these teenagers were.

Source: Ananova

JAILHOUSE LAWYER

All right, this one's pretty much the height of stupidity. It's June 2003. A lawyer is going to visit his clients at the Cook County Jail. He figures, you know, as long as I'm going, I might as well get them something nice to share with their new friends in the jail yard. Because, let's face it, you can never be too popular in jail! Maybe some cookies or some inspirational tracts ("Proverbs for Prisoners")?

Guess again. Try a quarter pound of weed, taped to the lawyer's thighs.

Our lawyer, who *really* ought to have known better, tried to get the pot past the drug-sniffing dogs at the jail. Hey, the reason they call them "drug-sniffing dogs" is because that's what they *do*. And that's what they did, raising the alarm by barking up a storm as the lawyer entered the jail. At this point the lawyer chose not to offer up any excuses—such as "I wore this suit to a Dave Matthews concert" or "My glaucoma's been acting up again"—and allowed a search. The pot was found, and he was arrested on charges of bringing contraband into a penal institution. And that's a felony, with a sentence of up to five years.

So boys and girls, just say no.

Here's some irony for you: although the lawyer admitted he was bringing in the pot to give to his clients, none of his clients were charged, because the pot never made it to them. Not that they should get too smug. The lawyer posted bail and they're still in the slammer.

Source: Associated Press

TAKE A BITE OUT OF CRIME

Here's a lesson about sticking body parts where you oughtn't to. "Goran" was weaving his way drunkly down a street in Zagreb, Croatia, when he decided to harass a woman standing in her yard. At first he cursed and shouted at her, but it wasn't giving him any satisfaction. So Goran stumbled over to the woman's property, dropped trou, and stuck Little Goran through the fence. What Goran didn't realize in his drunk, harassing state was that she wasn't alone.

Snausages! Snausages!
With her was her dog "Medo," which we are told means "Little Bear" in Croat. Well, Little Bear saw what came through the fence and, either motivated by Goran's lack of manners or sensing the opportunity for a little snack, went right up to the offending appendage and took a bite—although fortunately for Goran, the dog did not actually manage to take a bite out.

This is where it gets good: Goran filed a police report! The police were not notably sympathetic; yes, he had a nasty bite on a rather sensitive part of his body, but if he hadn't been acting like a jerk, both he and Little Goran would have made it through the night unscathed. Goran was charged with "insulting the moral feelings of citizens" and "violation of public order." As for Medo, he probably spent the next couple of days dragging his tongue across the dirt to get the taste out of his mouth.

Source: Reuters

GIVE 'EM 15 MINUTES AND YOU'LL HAVE THE SCREENPLAY FOR *GIGLI*

Thomas Huxley is supposed to have said that if you gave an infinite number of monkeys an infinite number of typewriters, eventually they would produce the works of William Shakespeare.

Researchers at Plymouth University in England, armed with dauntless curiosity about typing monkeys, and, not entirely coincidentally, taxpayer money, gave a computer to six macaques in the Paignton Zoo in southwest England in early 2003, to see what prose, if any, these monkeys might commit to the computer screen.

Here's the Poop

The results, shall we say, were not *entirely* unexpected. Once presented with the computer, the alpha male of the monkeys, apparently having recently caught *2001: A Space Odyssey* on basic cable, picked up a rock and started smashing his new monolith. The rest of the monkeys, not nearly as ambitious, merely defecated on the keyboard. After a month of coexistence with this miracle of high technology, the six macaques had typed five pages of text—mainly the letter "S" with occasional appearances of "J," "L," "M," and, for vowel purposes, "A." No Shakespeare. Heck, not even any Gertrude Stein.

The lead researcher for the project said that it did have some benefit: "It showed that monkeys are not random generators. They're more complex than that."

It also showed that if you give a monkey a computer, you damn well better have the thing professionally cleaned afterward.

Purists will note that the experiment was doomed from the start: Huxley called for infinite monkeys, each with his or her own personal Underwood, not six macaques time-sharing a word processor for 30 days. Anyone who has to share a computer with someone else knows how hard it is to get any work done with someone constantly looking over your shoulder. What this experiment really shows is this: even lower primates get writer's block.

Ol' Will Shakespeare would probably sympathize.

Source: Associated Press

* * *

"[Computer] programming today is a race between software engineers striving to build bigger and better idiot-proof programs, and the Universe trying to produce bigger and better idiots. So far, the Universe is winning."

—**Rich Cook**

"To err is human; to remain in error is stupid."

—**Anonymous**

PAY FOR TV?
THAT'S COMMUNISM!

This might be shocking to Americans, but in Britain, you have to pay to watch TV. The British government charges its subjects annually for the privilege of staring blankly in the direction of dancing electrons; in 2003, the fee was £116 (about $185). Now, *why* Americans, two-thirds of whom live in households that are hooked up to cable television of some sort, would find paying for TV shocking is another question entirely. Nevertheless, there it is.

Not every person in the United Kingdom complies with the license fee; an estimated 2 million of the queen's subjects refuse to pay. The British government doesn't just sit idly by, though. Why, if the masses start getting used to the idea of free telly, anarchy would surely follow!

Big BBC Is Watching
To prevent citizens from freeloading their BBC, an agency called TV Licensing tours the countryside in special detector vans that pick up a signal that U.K. televisions emit when they're turned on. If they catch a signal coming from someplace that doesn't have a license, the unlicensed cable poachers get hauled into court, where they could be charged up to £1,000 in fines.

Leaving aside the issue of whether charging people to watch TV is dumb, and the fact that having people driving around your neighborhood tracking your television usage is Orwellian in a profoundly bad sort of way, let us grant that if you're nabbed illegally watching TV in Britain, you better have a really good excuse as to why the Beeb's on the box without your quids paid to the queen.

But We Only Watch Reruns

As you might expect, good excuses are in short supply, but bad ones are plentiful. TV Licensing has collected some of their favorite excuses. They are, in no particular order:

"That's not a TV you saw through the window. It's just my Christmas tree lights!"

"How did that TV get in here? I've never seen it before in my life!"

"We don't watch the TV. We just keep it around to give the cat somewhere to sleep."

And our favorite:

"I thought if I wrapped my TV up in kitchen foil, your detector vans wouldn't be able to detect it."

Silly people. Everyone knows that kitchen foil only works to prevent the aliens from beaming messages *into* your TV, not keeping signals from coming *out* of it.

Source: *Scotsman*, TV Licensing

* * *

"It's so simple to be wise. Just think of something stupid to say and then don't say it."

—Sam Levenson

TIPS FOR STUPID CRIMINALS

Because you never know when one of these guys might pay attention.

THAT DIVAN LOOKS DIVINE
Today's tip: Try to stay fresh.

Burglar "Rob" lurked on the streets of Amsterdam. Make no mistake, it's a strenuous gig: all that skulking, sneaking, and burgling is very physical work. And it had its effect on Rob.

In August 2003 he snuck into a nice old lady's house and stole some of her jewelry. But then all his thievery sapped him of his will to go on. The nice old lady's sofa beckoned, so cozy, so soft. Rob lay down and within minutes was off in a refreshing slumber.

Refreshing, that is, until he found himself being nudged awake by the cops; the nice old lady had found him snoozing on the sofa and made the call. Lying there on the sofa, the old woman's jewelry still in his hands, Rob didn't even bother to try to come up with an excuse for being in someone else's house with someone else's property. He just owned up to the theft and gave himself up. We hope he'll get some rest in jail.

Source: Reuters

* * *

"What people commonly call fate is mostly their own stupidity."

—**Arthur Schopenhauer**

THE U.S. FLAG:
LOVE IT OR MOVE TO NORWAY!

I n the United States, it's not illegal to burn the national flag in protest. It's not good flag etiquette and it's not especially smart, since you may be pummeled by burly people whose understanding of constitutional protections is limited to the lyrics of Lee Greenwood's trot-it-out-in-wartime chestnut "God Bless the USA." But technically, it's legal. Even the Supreme Court says so (Texas v Johnson, 1989), and the Supreme Court isn't exactly staffed with Commies, you know.

Accidentally on Purpose
Norwegian comedian Otto Jespersen didn't think he would have a problem when he burned a U.S. flag on his satirical comedy show *Torsdagsklubben* (*The Thursday Club*) in February 2003. The burning flag was part of a sketch in which Jespersen appeared to endorse the then-imminent U.S.-led war with Iraq by lighting a candle. Jespersen put the candle on a desk, where it "accidentally" set fire to a U.S. flag flying nearby. What can we say? It's Norwegian humor.

Crime and Punishment Norwegian Style
Ironically, it would have been better for Jespersen if he'd burned that flag on the very steps of the U.S. Capitol. Because in Norway it's honestly and genuinely against the law: Paragraph 95 of Norway's criminal code expressly forbids insulting a foreign state's flag. So in Norway, you can't burn the U.S. flag, shred it,

use it as a diaper, or even go up to it and tell it that all those vertical stripes make it look *really fat.* That's insulting. And in Norway, that's a crime.

As a result, Jespersen and his show's producer, Kaare Valebrokk, were formally charged with burning the U.S. flag. They might have spent up to a year in prison, but they ended up with a fine instead. That's what you get for not knowing your own nation's laws, and that's more than they would have gotten, say, in Texas. Maybe next time, they should do a location shot. Texans *love* that kind of edgy humor!

Source: *Aftenposten*

* * *

"BIG, FLABBY BUTTOCKS" BANNED IN THAILAND

Bad news for hefty world travelers? No, but not so good for karaoke singers: it is one of three songs (along with "I Fear No Sins" and "I Do Fear Sins") banned from Thai radio and TV for promoting immorality among the Thai. "In society, does freedom of speech mean we have to talk only about sex?" asked Pramoj Rathavinij, deputy director general of Thailand's Public Relations Department. Pramoj, my man, if you have to ask.

Source: Reuters

COPS! LIVE ON MTV!

Fans of the mystery genre will tell you that the perfect crime is unheard of because it requires that the perpetrator never talk about it. You know that people just can't shut up about things like that. ("Dude, I did *so* commit the perfect crime and I'll show you where I hid the body to prove it!") So think about how much easier it is to talk about an *imperfect* crime, especially when there's a TV camera.

Bad Brad

Nineteen-year-old "Brad" found himself in front of an MTV camera, and before you know it, he was confessing his crimes to a national audience—on a few occasions he'd taken a baseball bat to mailboxes in his hometown of Eaton, Connecticut. It's not the perfect crime—heck, it's not even an *interesting* crime—and that may be why Brad felt free to proclaim his own bad self.

Sadly for Brad, it seems that the boys in blue down at Eaton Police Department watch MTV. (It's part of the effort by law enforcement to keep tabs on Carson Daly, and to decide whether "fo' shizzle my nizzle" actually means anything you can get arrested for.) The cops caught Brad confessing his crimes and crafted a warrant for his arrest.

So remember, kids: MTV is for music, not confessing criminal activity. If you must admit to criminal activity on TV, do it where no one's watching. VH1 is good.

Source: Associated Press

GIVE HIM A PINK SLIP

I magine for a moment that you are an assistant store manager for a large grocery chain in the Southern U.S. (unless you actually are an an assistant store manager for a large grocery chain in the South. In which case, don't imagine it. Just be who you *are*, man). There you are, doing whatever it is assistant managers do, when you get a phone call. It's from someone claiming to be with the police, who tells you that you need to call in one of your store employees and strip search her—and don't worry, since he's from the police, you're duly authorized.

Do you:

    a) Chuckle, say, "Yeah, I'll get *right* on that," and then continue price checking peas.

    b) Call in said store employee, tell her to strip, take away her clothes, and force her to pose, opening yourself up to arrest and your grocery store chain to a big, fat, lawsuit.

If you picked "a" then you are not "Allen," an assistant manager at a Winn-Dixie store in Panama City, Florida. In July 2003, Allen, on the advice and counsel of the "policeman" on the phone, made one of his employees strip and strike poses, and was not particularly hasty about giving her clothes back, according to police.

Time for a Career Change

After the woman got her clothes back, she contacted the police, who visited Allen and put him in the express arrest line (five charges or less!), charging him with false imprisonment and lewd and lascivious behavior. He was released on $10,000 bail, which one assumes could not be reduced with the judicious use of a Winn-Dixie Reward Card.

The "policeman" on the other end of the phone was a prankster whose existence was well known to the real police. Lt. Claude Arnold of the Panama City police told the Associated Press that his department had been receiving complaints about similar calls for the last five years, and indeed had been alerted by law enforcement in North Dakota just a week earlier that similar calls had been made to stores in that state from pay phones in Panama City.

In a general sense, taking a caller's word that he's a police officer is probably no smarter than responding to a query as to whether or not the store has Prince Albert in a can. As Lt. Arnold noted: "Who would trust a cop over the phone like that?" Now we know.

Source: Associated Press

* * *

AND YOU THOUGHT YOUR WORK BREAK WAS SHORT?

Argentinean news agency *Diarios y Noticias* reported that a grocery store in Argentina's western Mendoza province required female cashiers to wear adult diapers. The idea was presented as a preventative measure to keep them from taking breaks, or in case "cold, nerves, pressure, or stress" caused them to lose bladder control.

Source: Reuters

TIPS FOR STUPID CRIMINALS

We keep writing these, but they just won't listen.

BECAUSE I LOOK GOOD IN PUMPS
Today's tip: Wear appropriate footwear.

The first clue the Soerum, Norway, police had that something was amiss was a 19-year-old guy trying to run from the scene of a crime in black high-heel shoes. The man was otherwise not in drag, so his choice of footwear seemed, well, *odd.* So they asked him: "What's with the shoes?" He had no good answer, not even to suggest that in fact they were *incredibly* comfortable and that he suspected all the young dudes would be wearing them soon.

Things became a little clearer when they entered the Soerum City Hall—the scene of the crime—and found a pair of tennis shoes, which coincidentally were the right size for our pump-loving guy. Seems the guy was bright enough to want to cover his tracks by wearing someone else's shoes (police suspect he found the pumps in the office), but not so bright that he remembered to take his own shoes with him when the alarm sounded and he took off.

Eventually, our footwear fiend admitted to breaking into city hall and vandalizing the place by spraying graffiti on the walls. His punishment should probably be to keep wearing those high heels. But then they might clash with his jumpsuit. And wouldn't that be a crime?

Source: Reuters

PAGING SENATOR RYDER

In June 2003, the U.S. Senate was considering adding a rule to its operating procedures: *Don't steal the furniture*.

It didn't actually say it that way, but what it did say was that members of the U.S. Senate shouldn't remove furniture, paintings, or other historic items. Some of these items manage to get labeled as "surplus," at which point the senator buys it for a bargain basement amount, but some of these items just plain disappear, often, one suspects, after a senator is voted out of office. As if that cushy Senate pension wasn't enough.

The new rule, which was introduced by Senator Christopher Dodd of Connecticut, would create a list of items that senators would be specifically forbidden to snatch, including art and objects with historical value. Presumably you could still sneak out with a stapler or two, provided it wasn't Lyndon Johnson's stapler before it was yours.

Senator Trent Lott of Mississippi, who chaired the U.S. Senate Rules Committee, noted that he expected the rule resolution to pass, and a good thing, too: "There has been no real restraint," he said. He also noted that at the time the rule was recommended "most of the good stuff" from the early days of the nation had already been carted away.

Source: Reuters

50,000 VOLTS IS JUST GOD'S WAY OF TELLING YOU TO PLAY THROUGH

Golfers know that thunderstorms and golfing simply don't mix. There's a good reason for this. Place a golfer, even a short one, on the relatively flat, rolling plain that is a golf course, and he instantly becomes the tallest object for yards around. Lightning always tries to seek the shortest distance between its cloud and the ground. Add to this the fact that golfers are swinging the sports world's equivalent of lightning rods every time they hit the ball toward the green, which in a thunderstorm is just like daring God to take a crack at you. It's not smart. If lightning can hit Lee Trevino, it can hit you.

Not Smart Enough to Come in out of the Rain
"Sam" loved his golf. Sam loved his golf so much that when it started thundering while he was playing a round at the Orton Meadows Golf Course in Peterborough, Cambridgeshire, in May 2003, he stayed on the course, using an umbrella to keep himself dry as he waited for his shots. On the 14th hole, while he was waiting for the rain to let up, Mother Nature sent a message to Sam to call it a day: she zapped him. Lightning hit his umbrella and went coursing up his arm. Most people would take a few thousand volts up the ulna as a sign to get back to the clubhouse, but not Sam. Sam played through.

Hey! I'm Talking to You

Mother Nature, apparently miffed, rang Sam back: on the 17th hole, Sam was *struck by lightning again*—once again, his umbrella acted as a lightning rod and poured lightning into his umbrella-wielding appendage. But Sam was not deterred. He'd made it to the 17th hole and by God he would finish the round. After all, the chances of being struck by lightning twice are more than three million to one. With those sorts of odds, maybe he'd get lucky.

He *was* lucky, to the extent that a third bolt of lightning did not sizzle down from the sky and strike him. His score, alas, was not nearly as electrifying. "I won't tell you my score. It was a bad day," he told reporters. "But I don't think that was anything to do with the lightning. I just had a stinker."

Sam is ready to play again. His only problem now is no one wants to join him in a foursome.

Source: Ananova

* * *

"A word to the wise ain't necessary; it's the stupid ones who need the advice."

—Bill Cosby

SOMETIMES THE INSECT WINS

There are a lot of things you can do naked—and as a subset of that, there are things you *can* do naked, but probably *shouldn't*. One of those things, in our humble opinion, is riding a motorcycle. Why? Two words: road rash.

There are other reasons, too, as "Erich" discovered while he was driving his hog around the German nudist colony where he was staying. Erich wasn't totally nude—he was wearing sunglasses, a scarf, and sandals—but he was nude enough that when a small, angry bee came right at him, it had an unobstructed shot at, well, let's just say a normally *protected* area. Fortunately the bee missed, but not by much; Erich got stung on the inner thigh. In all the excitement and confusion and venomous pain, Erich lost control of his motorcycle and flew off it.

It Could Have Been a Nasty Scrape

Stop wincing; despite the potential for leaving more of himself on the road than on his bones, Erich emerged from his calamity with a mere shoulder injury and some bumps and bruises (and, of course, a bee sting). That's one lucky naked motorcycle-riding German. Although maybe not so lucky after all: when the police arrived at the scene of the accident, they debated whether or not to ticket Erich. Not because he was naked, mind you, but because he wasn't wearing a helmet.

Source: Ananova

STUPID AIR TRAFFIC CONTROLLER TRICKS

In June 2003, the leaders of the G-8 countries (France, the United States, the United Kingdom, Germany, Japan, Italy, Canada, and Russia) were meeting in Evian, France, on the shores of Lake Geneva. The airspace over the meeting site naturally was restricted—it wouldn't do to have an aerial attack on the world's most powerful people.

As it so happens, one French transport helicopter *did* briefly enter into the restricted airspace. In one of those moments of air controller wit (or possibly extreme boredom), a Swiss air traffic controller jokingly labeled the errant helicopter "Al Qaeda" on his radar screen. We imagine he then called over all of his coworkers and they had a nice chuckle. To a Swiss air traffic controller, there's nothing funnier than labeling French helicopters as terrorists.

Off the Radar

Thing is, that "Al Qaeda" label *also* showed up on the radar screens of the French military. Quicker than it takes to think about the fact that a real Al Qaeda helicopter probably *wouldn't* voluntarily identify itself as belonging to the most feared terrorist organization in the world, the French scrambled their Mirage jets to bring down the chopper. And they would have blasted it too, had not a last-minute correct identification revealed that the helicopter was French. The French, naturally, were not amused, and in retrospect, even the

Swiss air controller admitted what he'd done was "absolutely stupid." He was given some enforced time off pending a disciplinary hearing. Not good news for him, but at least it means he won't have another dull day at work for a while.

Source: Associated Press

* * *

PAGING HOMER

Sure, it's amusing when you watch *The Simpsons* and Homer is snoozing away blissfully at his nuclear power plant job. But in the real world, it's a little scary. So you won't be comforted to know that in June 2003, the sole operator in the control room of the MIT Nuclear Reactor Laboratory in Cambridge, Massachusetts, had an early morning catnap. His nap was discovered when his working partner was locked out for more than a half an hour and couldn't raise his pal by way of phone, pager, or radio. By the time the napper woke up, the police were on their way. Makes you feel safe, doesn't it?

Source: *Boston Globe*

* * *

"There are more fools in the world than there are people."

—**Heinrich Heine**

MON *DIEU!* STOP THE MUSIC!

V alerie Faure was both a French lawyer and an avid player of the accordion—two facts that, when combined, would make one suspect it would be impossible for her to find a spouse. Nevertheless, she was married to a man who played the violin. For fun and relaxation, the two liked to hang out on the street corners of their hometown of Bergerac and play their instruments for the amusement of passersby, who may or may not drop coins into their open music cases.

One day, two of those passersby happened to be French lawyers—French lawyers who became incensed that one of their own would be doing such a horrible, awful thing. Successfully defending potential criminals is one thing, but playing an accordion on the street, well, that was just très *sick*. French lawyers have a reputation to protect, and they're not above disbarring a lawyer when her conduct is unbecoming and unprofessional. Indeed, there's a rich tradition of French lawyers getting the boot for extracurricular activity. As far back as 1826, a French lawyer was disbarred for performing in the theater, because you can't have a lawyer as an actor. Actors are professional liars! And that's not like a lawyer at all.

And so Mme. Faure was hauled up in front of her local bar association, which suspended her from practicing law because of her penchant for playing the accordion on the street. But Faure—who was a lawyer, after all—filed an appeal and her perseverance paid off; her bar association's decision was overturned.

Interestingly, the decision noted that Faure couldn't have demeaned the profession of lawyer by her accordion playing because she wasn't wearing her lawyer's robes while she was performing. So all you French lawyers who like to perform in the street, just make sure you do it in casual attire. Also, based on this line of reasoning, the lawyer in the 1826 case has excellent grounds for appeal. Free the French lawyers!

Source: Agence France-Presse

* * *

MISSING THE POINT

A Russian tightrope walker was told to wear a hard hat while performing his act in Britain—this despite the fact that the man does his act without a net. Goussein Khamdoulaev, a performer with the Moscow State Circus, traded in his usual Cossack hat when the circus was told by insurers that it had to comply with new workplace rules put in place by the European Union. What value the hard hat would have if Khamdoulaev fell from the traditional tightrope height of 50 feet is unclear.

Source: London *Times*

THE TOILET PAPER–DISPENSING PDA COSTS EXTRA

One often overlooked aspect of a successful hoax is the willing suspension of disbelief on the part of those being hoaxed. At some fundamental level, most people who get hoaxed really, truly want to believe, and this desire to believe allows them to overcome logical objections that someone else might immediately see. Say, for instance, that Van Gogh did not in fact regularly work in the medium of Marks-A-Lot permanent markers or that Hitler's diaries probably weren't written in a lined, spiral notebook with Spongebob Squarepants on the cover.

Après the Internet Café
A perfect example of this willing suspension of disbelief occurred in April 2003, when tech journalists across the world reported that the British arm of Microsoft's MSN Internet service had created the world's first Internet-enabled portable toilet: the "iLoo." "The Internet is so much a part of everyday life now that surfing on the loo was the next natural step," opined MSN spokesperson Tracy Blacher. MSN was creating a self-contained waste station complete with a wireless keyboard, a plasma screen, and wi-fi Net access. Never had it been easier to do your business while you were doing your business. MSN declared that the new iLoos would debut at music festivals across England over the summer.

Hey Dude, Hurry Up with That Download

At this juncture, some of the less starry-eyed might have observed some of the following data points:

1. Longtime Microsoft rival Apple is the technology company that habitually names its products with a lowercase "i" out in front—"iMac," "iPod," "iBook," "iTunes"—so Microsoft trying to come out with an iAnything would be likely to arouse the iWrath of Apple's iLawyers. Therefore, it probably was not meant to be taken seriously.

2. As anyone who has ever gone to a summer concert knows, music festivals' portable toilets are a prime example of man's inhumanity to man. Using one for even a few seconds is unadulterated hell in a fiberglass shell; the idea that someone would want to hang out in one and check e-mail strains credulity.

3. Anyone who admits to downloading jpgs of anime chicks while a line full of sun-baked partiers are not so slowly becoming candidates for peritonitis is going to spend the rest of the concert trapped screaming in the portable toilet tank.

4. Two words to dissuade anyone from touching that keyboard: people miss.

But tech reporters, enticed by the idea of surfing the Web while riding the porcelain throne, reported it uncritically. It wasn't until a couple of weeks later that Microsoft admitted what should have been obvious: "I can confirm it was an April Fools' joke," said Microsoft spokesperson Nouri Bernard Hasan. Seems the British arm of MSN is filled with irrepressible pranksters who learned all they know from *Monty Python's Flying Circus*. It was a prank, nothing more.

Rebooting the System

Or was it? No sooner had Microsoft admitted fooling the media than it reversed itself: "We jumped the gun basically yesterday in confirming that it was a hoax and in fact it was not," said yet another Microsoft spokesperson. The line from Redmond now was that it wasn't really a hoax, but the point was moot, since the iLoo project was canceled anyway. To which the obvious rejoinder is "Okay, guys, whatever you say."

So who ends up looking dumber: the tech media, for breathlessly announcing the iLoo, or Microsoft, for announcing it, denying it, and then denying the denial? All one can truly say is that the portable toilets at the summer festivals aren't the only things that stink about this story.

Source: *USA Today*

* * *

"Before we work on artificial intelligence, why don't we do something about natural stupidity?"

—Steve Polyak

"If 50 million people believe a foolish thing, it is still a foolish thing."

—Anatole France

IF YOU'RE SEEING DOUBLE, DOES THAT MEAN YOU'VE VOTED TWICE?

There are all sorts of things you probably shouldn't do when you've been drinking. Driving is a big one, but so are (in no particular order) operating heavy machinery, signing legal documents, formalizing lifetime commitments, climbing over zoo fences to play with large mammals, and telling your in-laws what you *really* think about them.

Voting while drunk is another bad idea. People do a bad enough job of it sober, after all; the idea of people stumbling into the voting booth and trying to operate one of those little punch pens is enough to terrify even those folks who have somehow managed to wrap their minds around the concept of an electoral college.

Arriving Under the Influence

For these reasons among others (although not so much the electoral college thing), Norway has long outlawed voting while drunk. Indeed, the Norwegian law specifically bars voters entry to voting booths if they exhibit "reduced consciousness" or "seriously impaired judgment." One could of course argue that it's difficult to say whether one shows seriously impaired judgment until *after* one has made one's voting selections. But let's leave that alone for now. The point is if you're plastered in Norway, you're not voting.

I Demand My Rights As a Citizen!

Or, at least, you weren't voting. But now comes news that, for the 2004 general elections at least, Norwegians will be able to vote while blasted. "The election board can no longer refuse anyone to vote because they are intoxicated," the local government ministry told the *Bladet Tromso* newspaper in July 2003. Meanwhile, Norwegian politicians, apparently alarmed at the prospect of all of Norway getting tanked and falling into the voting booths, have reinstated the "no drinking, no voting" law, but the new law won't take effect until 2005.

So we have one guaranteed year of drunken Norwegian voting! Sure, it's a bad idea—but it's a bad idea that's happening somewhere else. That's the best kind of bad idea.

Sources: *Bladet Tromso*, Reuters

* * *

FAIR'S FAIR

A policeman in the state of Victoria in Australia was wondering why female police officers were allowed to wear their hair long, but men were not. It didn't seem fair to him. So he complained. And it worked: the state police hair regulations were made "gender non-specific." So male officers are now allowed to wear their hair long. And interestingly, theoretically, female police officers are also allowed to wear beards and mustaches. Wonder how many will?

Source: *Herald-Sun* (Australia)

FOR GOD'S SAKE, DON'T GO AFTER A GRIZZLY WITH ENDUST

A fricanized honey bees, better known as the dreaded "killer bees," have a nasty if slightly overblown reputation. They're not waiting to jump you and steal your lunch money, but if you *do* disturb them, you'll find that they have shorter tempers and longer memories than their European-bred counterparts. Which is to say, they attack more quickly and will chase you farther distances than their more domesticated counterparts. Leave them alone and they'll generally leave you alone. However, if you go and intentionally tick them off, don't be at all surprised when they decide to live up to their name.

Let Us Spray

Just ask "Tom" of Las Vegas, who in May 2003 had been fighting an ongoing war with the hive of Africanized bees in his front yard for just about five years. From time to time Tom would hit the bees with bug spray, but the stubborn bees simply wouldn't take the hint. Tom decided it was time to escalate the attacks, and try a new form of chemical warfare: Comet cleanser.

Now, Comet does many things well, most of them, not surprisingly, having to do with cleaning. Procter & Gamble, which makes the popular product, suggests it for "tough cleaning problems around the house"—the kitchen, tub, and toilet bowl, for example. But nowhere on the packaging does it suggest that the

product would be excellent at rubbing out bees.
Perhaps Tom was an optimist. He took a handful of the
stuff and flung it into the bee hive.

Let's Get the Heck Outta Here!

This was rather quickly followed by the bees swarming
around Tom and stinging him viciously. "He was running all over the place trying to get them off his head
and he came in here and he fell on the ground," his
neighbor Shirley Collura told a local television station.
Perhaps the bees were insulted by the implicit suggestion they were unhygienic and needed a good scrub-
bing. Perhaps they were irritated by the fact that
Comet's primary active ingredient, sodium dichloro-s-
triazinetrione dihydrate, does not really improve the
taste of honey. It may have simply been that after five
years of low-grade hostilities, the bees needed to show
Tom that just because you have opposable thumbs and
cleansers doesn't mean you're the boss.

Whatever the reason, it was the bees who cleaned
Tom's clock, not the other way around. "I grabbed a
handful of [Comet] and put it in that hole and I never
should have done it," Tom said later, and probably
painfully.

Incidentally, here's a note from your can of Comet:
"It is a violation of Federal law to use this product in a
manner inconsistent with its labeling." So not only
were Tom's actions dumb, they were also illegal. No
wonder the bees attacked.

Source: KLAS-TV

HAKENKREUZING FOR A BRUISING

ere's the basic rule on using swastikas in your decorating: don't. Crazy as it may seem, people still haven't stopped associating this particular symbol with genocidal Nazis bent on world domination.

But people still slip up, including some people who really ought to know better. For example, the Coca-Cola Company. In April 2003, Coke did a promotion in Hong Kong that featured a popular series of robotlike toys called Robocons. With the purchase of a six-pack of Coke and the equivalent of $3.60, you could take home one of several Robocon toys, complete with a plastic base emblazoned with the Coca-Cola logo. Among these characters was "Robowaru," a goofy-looking fellow with silvery boots, a headdress that looks like a melted motorcycle helmet, and two, count 'em, two swastikas on his chest—one for each pectoral muscle.

Good vs. Evil

Now, it's true that they have swastikas in Asia whose arms point in the other direction. And they are symbols of peace! Buddhist-style swastikas are common all over our largest continent. However, in this particular case, close examination reveals that the arms of Robowaru's swastikas do not point in the happy, prosperous, riding-high-on-the-eternal-wheel-of-rebirth direction, but in the evil, let's-blitzkrieg-though-Europe direction. It's the little details that make the difference.

To Coke's defense, the cola giant did not create Robowaru—the toys were made to specifications provided by the Robocon designers. But you'd think *someone* would have noticed. The person who eventually did notice was Hong Kong-based rabbi Yakkov Kermaier. He said that while he believed it was an innocent enough flub, the toy and its attendant swastikas still had to go. "It's not simply a politically incorrect symbol," he noted. "It's an emblem that represents the wholesale slaughter of six million Jews."

Coca-Cola agreed and pulled the Robowaru figure from stores in late April. That's the good news. The bad news, of course, is now that particular figurine is certain to become a collector's item.

Source: Associated Press

* * *

A MAN WALKS INTO A DENTIST'S OFFICE

Man: "Excuse me, can you help me? I think I'm a moth."

Dentist: "You don't need a dentist. You need a psychiatrist."

Man: "Yes, I know."

Dentist: "So why did you come in here?"

Man: "The light was on."

OM, OM, OW!

Yoga can help you relax, make you feel more calm, reduce your stress level, and possibly even help you extend your life. Unless, that is, you decide that yoga can help you avoid a shark attack while you're standing in shark-infested waters. In which case, let us suggest that yoga is possibly more dangerous than driving drunk while smoking crack.

We know you're skeptical. So we invite you to meet Dr. Erich Ritter, a behavioral scientist who was under the impression that by using certain yoga techniques, he would be able to hang out with the bull sharks who live in Walker's Cay in the Bahamas and not be molested, even though the waters in which he stood had been liberally laden with chunks of cut-up fish. The doctor's thinking was that through yoga, he could slow his heartbeat and calm himself to the point where the sharks would see him as just another predator. He also suggested to the Discovery television network crew who accompanied him that he could read shark body language, which is what kept him from being nibbled on in the past.

So what happened? Well, what do you think?

Somebody Call a Doctor!
The damn fool got bit, of course; a shark ripped off his left calf. It was aiming for a remora fish that darted between Dr. Ritter's legs in an attempt to avoid being eaten. And indeed, the shark missed the remora. Good strategy on the remora's part, but very bad news for Ritter, who was now bleeding like crazy in shark-filled

water, and who suffered massive blood loss and had to be rushed back to Florida for a six-week stay in the hospital. All of which was filmed by the Discovery network crew, who had a front row seat and who made a special out of it—"Anatomy of a Shark Bite." Really, there are easier ways to get on TV.

Defenders of Dr. Ritter may note that the doctor was sort of bitten on a technicality, since the shark was aiming for something else and Dr. Ritter just happened to be in the way. So there may still be something to the yoga-as-shark-repellent thing; at the very least, it wasn't definitively disproven. But we would imagine that's cold comfort when there's a fearsome ocean predator gnawing on your leg, for whatever reason. We'll be doing our yoga exercises on dry land, thank you very much.

Source: *Western Daily Press* (Bristol, UK)

* * *

THE MONEY! IT'S HAUNTED!

We know some of you persist in believing in psychics, even after Miss Cleo didn't see the Feds coming right at her, but trust us when we provide you with this handy tip: when your "psychic" tells you your cash is cursed and must be "cleansed," it's a scam. A Colorado woman found that out after handing over $5,000 in cash and a $33,000 check to her psychic to be karmically scoured, only to go to the psychic's apartment a few days later and find it cleaned out. The erstwhile psychic was tracked down and arrested; authorities know she scammed other people but they're too embarrassed to come forward. You didn't need to be psychic to figure that one out.

Source: TheDenverChannel.com

CONFIDENTIAL
COMMUNICATION GONE WRONG

S o there you are at work, flipping burgers, realigning the nuclear accelerator magnets, or whatever it is you do for a living, when you mention in passing to your boss that you're going to head over to the bank to deposit your paycheck. Your boss then scribbles out a note, hands it to you, and tells you not to read it but to give it to the teller when you get to the bank. Do you read it or not?

"Marty" can tell you why you should. He and three other employees of a North Carolina auto shop were on their way to the bank to salt away their hard-earned cash when (so one of the men says), their supervisor "Chet" gave Marty a note to hand over to the teller, instructing him not to read it. Marty, apparently a trusting soul who thought perhaps his boss needed coin wrappers or something, took the note and, as requested, handed it over to the teller unread. Upon receiving the note, bank employees read something along the lines of "This is a robbery. I've got a gun." So they handed over a box, which happened to contain $4,500 and an exploding ink canister.

The Joke's on You—and So Is the Ink

Neither Marty nor his pals thought anything was amiss until they left the bank and the exploding ink canister did its thing. "It was just like smoke started coming out of the box, and I said, 'Man, drop that box. There's money in it,'" one of the guys told the local newspaper. "I went around front to go into the bank, to let them know it was a mistake, but it was too late." Sensibly, everyone waited around for the cops to arrive.

Poor Marty was arrested for robbery with a dangerous weapon (even though no such weapon was displayed at the time) and Chet, who wrote the note, was charged with conspiracy to commit robbery. Marty's coworkers suggested the note had been a joke. We're guessing Marty and Chet aren't finding it very amusing. And if it was a joke, we sure hope Marty's jail stay counts as overtime. Or, perhaps hazard pay.

Source: *News & Observer* (Raleigh, NC)

* * *

NICK IT LIKE BECKHAM

Supermarkets are used to dealing with shoplifters stuffing candy bars or Christmas hams down their pants and then trying to walk out of the store, but over in the United Kingdom, supermarket chain Tesco wasn't expecting people to try to nick an entire human being. Or a cardboard cutout of him, anyway: seems that fervent fans of soccer superstar David Beckham snuck off with a number of life-sized cardboard Beckhams, used to promote the athlete's biography. The solution: cameras focused on the cutouts 24 hours a day, not to mention security alarms. Which suggests it might be a fine time to graze Tesco's candy aisle.

Source: ABC News Online (Australia)

LATER IN THE DAY, THE NRA WENT THROUGH THE HALLS SHOOTING BLANKS

The object of a doctors' lobbying group is to convince legislators to rally to doctors' causes, not to send them screaming through the halls of state government, convinced they've been infected with some horrible viral contagion.

The distinction between these two goals appears to have escaped the Florida College of Emergency Physicians. In May 2003, the group wanted to impress upon Florida state legislators the idea that medical malpractice insurance rates were reaching ridiculous heights, possibly driving doctors out of business. And that meant if some horrible disease suddenly struck Florida there might not be enough doctors to deal with problem.

Fair enough, good point. No doctors equals runaway viral infections equals lots of German tourists deciding that maybe this year they'll skip Epcot. It's just that the Florida College of Emergency Physicians chose an odd way to make this point to state legislators. The organization sent them all little toy petri dishes, which were meant to imply that if such a dish actually contained a virus, they'd all be in big trouble.

They Were Petri-fied
Unfortunately for the Florida College of Emergency Physicians, a number of legislators actually *believed* the petri dishes were filled with something contagious. Let's remember the Great Anthrax Scare of 2001, in

which the weaponized, sheep-killing microscopic nasty actually *did* show up on the desk of Senator Tom Daschle as well as in several other places—and killed a few innocent bystanders.

State legislators had every right to be just a *teensy* bit paranoid, which is why several called the Florida senate sergeant at arms about the little dishes, who in turn brought in the Florida Department of Law Enforcement. Police investigators pronounced the petri dishes harmless, other than their ability to cause a few panic attacks. That assessment also neglects the fact that it undoubtedly put the physicians' legislative effort on life support. Nothing puts you on a legislator's bad side like the feeling you've just exposed him to something that will turn his pancreas into Jell-O.

Maybe for their next act, the Florida College of Emergency Physicians might want to create a vaccine for stupid lobbying tricks.

Source: Associated Press

* * *

"Never attribute to malice what can be adequately explained by stupidity."
—**Nick Diamos**

DUMB MOVIE FESTIVAL: *THE ADVENTURES OF PLUTO NASH* (2002)

Our Entry: *The Adventures of Pluto Nash*, starring Eddie Murphy and Randy Quaid

The Plot (Such As It Is): Eddie Murphy plays a bar owner on the moon whose territory is muscled in on by the mob. Refusing the proverbial "offer you can't refuse" to sell his bar (after which the bar blows up), Murphy then runs about the lunar surface plotting his revenge, trailed by comedy relief in the form of a robotic Randy Quaid. That Quaid should be comedy relief for Eddie Murphy tells you what sort of trouble this picture is in; it's the sort of film that spends millions on special effects but forgets gravity on the moon is one-sixth that on Earth.

Fun Fact: The film was on the shelf at Warner Bros.'s studio for two years before it was finally released, with little fanfare, in August 2002. The ostensible excuse was that they were working on the special effects all that time. Yeah, that's it.

Total North American Box Office: $4,411,102 (source: The-Numbers.com). A record-setting bomb, considering the estimated budget of $100 million.

The Critics Rave!

"*The Adventures of Pluto Nash* is so unremittingly awful that labeling it a dog probably constitutes cruelty to canines . . . Watching it is like watching 90 minutes of outtakes—deleted scenes randomly assembled by a drunken night watchman at the studio."—*New York Post*

"In a sense, *The Adventures of Pluto Nash* does America a real service: Every generation needs its own hugely expensive yet unfathomably bad science fiction comedy flop, and it's not likely that Generation Y even remembers *Howard the Duck*. So now that *Pluto's* on the scene, we're good through 2015 at least."—*Dayton Daily News*

"*The Adventures of Pluto Nash* is so thoroughly drab that I wish it were worse. Awful movies have more personality than this."—*The Coast* (Halifax)

"The mystifying thing about the atrocity that is *The Adventures of Pluto Nash* is the puzzling question as to why this project attracted so many notable names in the first place. Did someone's Mercedes have to be paid off immediately or something?"—MovieEye.com

"It might be the first sci-fi comedy that could benefit from a *Three's Company*–style laugh track."—*Chicago Tribune*

"There are worse movies, but that's no excuse . . . rarely has so much money delivered so little entertainment."
—*TV Guide*

A SNAFU AT HQ

After the U.S. Armed Forces invaded Iraq and squashed the existing army, it fell upon the land's new overlords (the Americans) to create a new Iraqi army, one that was better run, better organized, and more inspiring to the average man on the street. And thus was born the New Iraqi Corps!

It was inspiring but not the way the U.S. authorities had hoped. Here's why. Make an acronym of "New Iraqi Corps" in English and you get "NIC." Depending on your age and inclinations, it might remind you of either a shaving mishap or a member of the Backstreet Boys. Neither is a big positive, but neither is so bad either.

But translate "New Iraqi Corps" into Arabic and make an acronym out of that, and you get something a little more . . . spicy. How spicy? Well, let's just say that if there were a U.S. SCUBA military unit called the Fabulous Underwater Corps, it'd have basically the same problem in English as the New Iraqi Corps has in Arabic.

One senior American official put it this way: "I am told reliably but unanimously that that acronym is not a nice word in Arabic. Therefore we had to come up with another word." This is why the New Iraqi Corps are now the New Iraqi Army, whose acronym means little in English and presumably even less in Arabic.

Incidentally, if there were a Fabulous Underwater Corps, we would have joined up long ago. Their gear would have been stunning.

Source: ABC News Online (Australia)

DUM-PL8S

In the United States the various states make a lot of money selling "personalized" license plates. If people stopped to think about it, they'd realize that, in reality, since every license plate has a different number on it, they are *all* personalized. Maybe "CBF 1134" doesn't say as much as "HOTDUDE" or "CUBZFAN," but on the other hand, if you think too much about the idea that one's entire life philosophy can be compressed into seven letters and numbers, you might go insane. However you look at it, it's a nice little profit center for your state government, and these days, they need every profit center they can get.

But these license-plate-based money-raising schemes have nothing on the license plate scheme that went on in Thailand. In that country, certain numbers are considered lucky, and there's a healthy black-market business selling lucky-numbered license plates to the rich and famous. Public complaints about this practice led Thailand's Land Transport Department to a decision to put lucky-numbered license plates up for auction and let people bid for them over three days in August 2003.

How High?

How much would you pay for a license plate you really wanted? $100? $200? $1,000? We hate to tell you, pal, but you're not even in the running. The plate with the luckiest number of all, "9999" (lucky because the number nine is associated with royalty), sold for $95,200—almost ten times the number on the plate.

"This is better than investing in the stock market," said plate winner Suriya Jungrungraungkit, in a comment that should alarm any investors in Far East securities. The next luckiest number, "5555," sold for $47,619. Of 42 "lucky" plates up for bid on the first day, the average bid was $23,900, or about three and a half times what the average Thai makes in a year.

That makes the guy driving around with the "CUBZFAN" plate seem like a financial genius.

Source: Associated Press

* * *

IT'S BETTER TO BE DRUNK IN NORWAY

A drunk driving case against an Oslo man was thrown out when it was discovered that the man's confession was extracted while he was drunk. And you're thinking, well, yeah. But apparently the police had no evidence the man had been drinking and driving other than his drunken confession, which was judged to be worthless because, after all, he was drunk at the time. We honestly don't know what to think about this.

Source: Aftenposten

* * *

"The doctrine of human equality reposes on this: that there is no man really clever who has not found that he is stupid."

—G. K. Chesterton

HE'S NOT EXACTLY HAPPY ABOUT THOSE "SKORTS," EITHER

Sometimes the world is just one seriously messed-up place. Besides famine, pestilence, and death, which we've been dealing with ever since our ancestors climbed out of the trees and thought it'd be a neat trick to stand on two legs, we've got other, newer problems as well: rapidly mutating superbugs, worldwide economic slumps, and of course, global warming.

The Seat of the Problem

Sure, we could have a UN conference where delegates from around the world intoned seriously about the root causes of all this unmitigated evil, but let's cut to the chase and come right out and state the real problem: pants. *Women's* pants.

Search your heart. You know it to be true. Women wearing pants is the center of our world's woes. At least according to the king of Swaziland, who said so in a national address in late May 2003. Quoth the king: "The Bible says curse be unto a woman who wears pants, and those who wear their husband's clothes. That is why the world is in such a state today."

Of course, now it's *clear*. If history shows us anything, it's that nothing bad ever happened until that meddlesome Amelia Bloomer popularized pants for women in the 1850s.

Ignore Him and Maybe He'll Go Away

Not everyone was convinced by the king, even in Swaziland. Reuters news agency asked women in Swaziland's capital of Mbabane what they thought. "The king says I am the cause of the world's problems because of my outfit. Never mind terrorism, government corruption, poverty, and disease, it's me and my pants. I reject that," one said.

Undoubtedly she was wearing pantaloons at the time.

Source: Reuters

* * *

SENIORS IN SENSIBLE SHOES

Australia's leading relationship counseling body has a suggestion to older women who have outlived their husbands and are worried about burying another man: try a woman instead. "As they get over 60, opportunities to get a man diminish substantially. Men marry younger women and they die about eight years younger, so there is a real male shortage," said Relationships Australia spokesman Jack Carney. "And as women get even older it gets much worse, so we ask them to entertain the idea of lesbian relationships."

Source: *Sunday Herald Sun*

* * *

"'Tis better to be silent and be thought a fool, than to speak and remove all doubt."

—**Mark Twain**

GRANDFATHER CLUCK

Grandpas like to be useful. And we have no doubt that being useful was what "Lars" intended, when he offered to pick up his 15-month-old grandson Jonas from day care in Copenhagen, Denmark.

Lars drove down to the day-care center, identified himself as Jonas's grandpa, and announced he was there to take the little cherub home. The day-care center staff handed over the tyke, and off Jonas and Lars went, back to Jonas's parents' place—where Lars discovered Jonas's mother already at home with another toddler. That toddler was Lars's grandson, Jonas. The toddler Lars had was someone else's kid, also named Jonas. What happened? Lars had gone to the wrong day-care center.

Bringing Down Baby

Lars drove back to the day-care center with the Jonas who was not his grandson, where he was greeted by the police, who'd been called by the panicked day-care staff after they realized they'd handed over the baby to someone they shouldn't have. Lars told his side of the story, and fortunately for him, he was believed. But we expect the day-care center might be looking at a lawsuit somewhere along the way.

As for Lars, we recommend that he spend more time with his grandson. You know, to make sure he knows what he looks like.

Source: Ananova

BLOODY DUMB

In July 2003, Ionel Bleoanca, a Romanian public prosecutor, was in a serious car accident. In critical condition, Bleoanca required a blood transfusion. His blood type was so rare that his doctors asked local blood banks to solicit donors.

Cut to the Turnu Severin prison, which holds dozens of criminals that Bleoanca helped put there. Prisons aren't noted for being wellsprings of human kindness, and prisoners aren't typically known to show any sort of kindness to the prosecutors that sent them up the river. In spite of that, more than 40 prisoners offered to give blood for Bleoanca.

A feel-good story of forgiveness and redemption? Remember, this book is called *Book of the Dumb*. And here comes the dumbness: this impromptu blood drive was rejected by the prison authorities, who said that even if one or more of the prisoners had the right blood type, they would not be allowed to donate blood to him. "We would have to deal with an obvious moral dilemma in this case," prison chief Vasile Burcu said. From our perspective it seems the real moral dilemma is that the prison authorities would apparently rather let Bleoanca die than receive blood from an inmate.

Source: Ananova

FAN SERVICE

Y̲ou'll recall the voting controversy that rocked the United States to its core—no, not the 2000 presidential thing! We're talking about the final vote between Clay Aiken and Ruben Studdard on *American Idol.* As you may recall, Clay's fans complained that they couldn't get through on the phones, a glitch (if it *was* a glitch) that kept their man from the prize they thought he deserved.

You'll recall the uncertainty that gripped the nation: what would Clay's fans do next? Eventually we realized that the sort of people who enjoyed it when Clay sang "Bridge over Troubled Water" were not the sort to do anything more than pout.

Meanwhile in the Middle East . . .

Better that than what happened on an Arab variation of the show, called *Arab Superstar,* in August 2003. It was the semifinal episode of the show, and there were three contestants remaining, from Lebanon, Syria, and Jordan. At the end of the show, the contestant from Lebanon, a singer named Melhem Zein, got voted off the island (to mix our reality show metaphors).

Unlike Clay Aiken fans, Melhem Zein fans are not pouters, or if they are, that's just the preliminary stage to actual violence. As it happens, *Arab Superstar* was taped in Beirut, Lebanon, and the hometown audience was not pleased to have their contestant tossed. After the vote was announced, the studio audience didn't just gripe, it rioted. One of the audience members even tried to attack the Jordanian finalist, after which 60 members of Lebanon's Internal Security Forces jammed into the studio to reimpose calm. The finalists, neither from Lebanon, fainted in shock and had to be taken to the hospital.

Outside the TV studio, scores of angry Lebanese converged, waving pictures of their fallen hero and chanting "With our blood and souls, we sacrifice for you, Melhem!" They also converged on the Le Bristol Hotel, where the contestants were staying, and were agitated enough that Zein's dad had to make an appearance in an attempt to calm them down. Demonstrations were reported all over the country, and newspaper accounts had the army surrounding the television station.

Now, that's fan loyalty! Which you just don't see people doing for Clay. Or for Ruben, for that matter.

Sources: Reuters, *Lebanon Voice*

* * *

"With fame I become more and more stupid, which of course is a very common phenomenon."
—**Albert Einstein**

IF HE'D TAKEN THE ICE CREAM, HE'D PROBABLY BE LOOKING AT A FELONY

Here's a family that's going to have a fun holiday season: in late July 2003, "Chad," a growing boy of 18, stopped by his sister's house in Ruther Glen, Virginia. His sister's mother-in-law was there, and Chad asked if he could come on in and look for a pair of sunglasses he'd left behind. Well, sure; into the house Chad went.

A couple of hours later, Chad's sister (let's call her "Debbie"), her husband, and the aforementioned mother-in-law decide they'd like something to eat. The husband suggests pizza, which they have in their freezer. Or do they? An examination of the freezer shows it to be pie free. Well then, says Debbie (or words to that effect), let's have some teriyaki chicken instead, I know that's in the freezer. Only it's not; it too is missing. The family is reduced to settling for scraps of indeterminate animal flesh pressed into a tube-like shape, i.e., hot dogs. But even these inferior sources of sustenance have gone missing. Debbie and her kin face the immediate prospect of starving, or at least having to order out.

Hey, Wait a Minute!
Then, a brain flash: Debbie remembers her mother telling her that Chad had scarfed down on pizza, teriyaki chicken, and hot dogs that very day! Debbie hied herself over to Mom's, where she found her

freezer bags. Armed with this evidence, Debbie confronted her brother, who denied everything. So Debbie called the cops, who carted Chad away and charged him with petty larceny. "They felt he needs to learn a lesson about taking other people's property," Sheriff's Capt. Scott Moser said to the *Fredricksburg Free Lance-Star*. Chad was still maintaining his innocence, though he also acknowledged "the facts look awful bad for me." Cut a deal with Debbie, Chad. Preferably sometime before the next family get-together.

No word on whether Chad actually found his sunglasses.

Source: *Fredericksburg Free Lance-Star*

* * *

EWE WILL LOVE THE TASTE

Thought you'd experienced every potato chip flavor known to man and beast? Guess again. In Scotland, they've developed haggis-flavored chips. The chips (or "crisps" as they're known there) are the brainchild of Jacqueline Raeside, a potato farmer looking to supplement her farm's income. And indeed, what better way than chips that taste of sheep's intestine? "These are our own flavors, and the recipes remain secret," Raeside said. Yes, "secret" is probably a good idea here. This is one food idea that's probably not going to make it across the ocean.

Source: Scotsman.com

TIPS FOR STUPID CRIMINALS

Brought to you by the letter "O," for "Obvious."

SMILE, YOU'RE ON CANDID STADIUM CAM
Today's tip: When wanted by the police, try not to get your mug plastered on the local baseball stadium's scoreboard.

I f "Andy," a 24-year-old parole violator also wanted on a drug-trafficking charge, had just followed that simple rule, he might still be out walking among us, violating his parole like a madman. Alas for him (but not for the rest of us), he did not. He was broadcast kissing his girlfriend on the "KissCam" at the Great American Ballpark, home of the Cincinnati Reds. His mug was seen by tens of thousands of hometown Reds fans, one of whom, as coincidence would have it, was Andy's parole officer. Shortly thereafter, the parole officer and a police officer deprived Andy of his front-row seats.

On the other hand, the Reds won the game, taking it from St. Louis 4–2. So it wasn't all bad.

Sources: Associated Press, Yahoo! Sports

* * *

"Never underestimate the power of human stupidity."
—**Robert Heinlein**

JEWELRY TO SPARE, APPARENTLY

Your jewelry store has roughly $800,000 worth of jewelry in its window display. That's quite a lot, even before the riotously high markup that is passed on to customers. Thus you feel the need to protect said jewelry from the people who might try to grab it and flee. Which of the following is not a good way to protect your expensive and sparkly trinkets?

1. Metal grilles: Designed to keep anything with an opposable thumb from reaching in and grabbing the jewelry in question—yes, even those crafty little spider monkeys you've heard so much about.

2. Armored glass: Go ahead! Hit it with a hammer! You just can't break it! Go on! All right, now stop. All that banging is going to give someone a headache.

3. State-of-the-art laser alarm system: Try as hard as you might, you can't move faster than a laser beam without breaking the laws of physics. And if you thought the penalties for breaking ordinary laws were bad, well, just you *wait*.

4. Cheap unprotected saw board roof: Put this over the display cases, unprotected by any of the three aforementioned protective measures —just right for sawing through, so a thief can reach down and scoop up the $800,000 in jewelry like it was just being given away!

Let's See . . . Decisions, Decisions

If you answered, "oh, number 4, definitely," then you might actually *be* one of the crooks who robbed a Munich jewelry store in early May 2003. The store owners had the laser alarm, metal grilles, and armored glass—and, unfortunately for them, the cheap unprotected wooden roof as well, through which the criminals sawed to steal the precious stones and gold rings.

A Munich police spokesman noted that "the roof over the display case window was not alarmed, but no one realized it. The alarm was only set up to work if the windows were broken." Our criminals, flouting the unspoken social contract that dictates they adhere to both verbs in the phrase "smash and grab," left the windows intact.

Next time, why not make it simpler? Just put the jewelry in a Tiffany bowl with a little sign that says "help yourself" calligraphed in gold on the front.

Source: Ananova

* * *

"For every complex problem, there is a solution that is simple, neat, and wrong."

—H. L. Mencken

"Nothing in all the world is more dangerous than sincere ignorance and conscientious stupidity."

—Martin Luther King Jr.

BALLOONATIC

Sometimes throwing water balloons is fun. And sometimes it's a federal offense. Wisdom comes from knowing the difference between the two.

"Chad," of Dixon, Illinois, was not particularly wise that summer day in 2003. At 33 years of age—an age at which one really ought to know better—he hurled a water balloon at the driver of an antique fire truck in the Dixon Petunia Festival Parade. Normally this would be chalked up to garden-variety obnoxiousness and forgotten. But it just so happened that the driver was Dennis Hastert, the Speaker of the House for the U.S. House of Representatives. Dixon also happens to be in his congressional district. So instead of it being ignored, Chad was arrested, charged with aggravated battery, and tossed in the clink until he coughed up $25,000 in bail.

Don't Even Think About Spraying the Vice President with Reddi-wip

In court, Chad explained that he didn't know he had thrown the water balloon at the Speaker of the House, or even at his own federal representative. Apparently he thought he was just heaving it at some random guy.

Judge Tomas Magdich was quick to enlighten him: "He is third in line to the presidency of the United States. You won't forget it next time, will you?" the judge said. Irony: the judge made a mistake. Hastert actually is second in line (the president, being president, doesn't count as being in line).

So the next time you are thinking of heaving a water balloon at someone, ask: "Do I know what my local federal representative looks like? And am I willing to make a federal case out of my right to launch water-filled latex projectiles?" If the answer to one or more of these questions is no, then be wise and hold your fire.

Source: Associated Press

* * *

FIGURES

From an Associated Press news article:
"A new panel charged with finding ways to make Connecticut government run more efficiently will release its report six months later than scheduled."

* * *

"The American people are very generous people and will forgive almost any weakness, with the possible exception of stupidity."

—**Will Rogers**

TIPS FOR STUPID CRIMINALS

*Because if we help them, maybe they can help themselves
(but not to our stuff).*

RESTRAIN YOURSELF
Today's tip: Your parole officer is not stalking you.

This is contrary to the point of view of "Evan," who in February 2003 asked for a temporary restraining order against a woman he described as a stalker, who was making him "depressed and in fear for my freedom." The temporary restraining order was granted—temporary restraining orders are often granted without investigation. It wasn't until later that it was discovered that the woman "stalking" Evan was his parole officer, who was merely trying to do her job. The restraining order was revoked, and Evan himself arrested for—you guessed it—not meeting with his parole officer. No doubt that the extra time in the can gave him a real reason to be depressed and in fear for his freedom.

Source: *Witchita Eagle*, "News of the Weird"

* * *

"In view of the fact that God limited the intelligence of man, it seems unfair that he did not also limit his stupidity."

—**Konrad Adenauer**

MAMA BEARS
DOWN ON THE CROWD

Here's the thing about pit bull terriers: they have a reputation for being twitchy, vicious bite machines. But as anyone who has ever owned an infamous breed of dog knows, most of the time the dog's actions have more to say about the intelligence of the owner than the dog's disposition.

With that in mind, our story begins in the Great Smoky Mountains National Park in Tennessee. It seems that on a July weekend a bunch of sightseers created what the locals call a "bear jam"—which means that they all stopped their cars and got out to *ooh* and *aah* at a mother bear and her three cubs. Among these sightseers was "Stanley," up from Georgia in his pickup with his pit bull.

Please Curb Your Dog

The Great Smoky Mountains National Park requires that dogs in the park be restrained. But wouldn't you know, Stanley apparently forgot about that, which would explain what happens next: his pit bull sized up one of the cubs, decided he could take it, and bolted from the road. Naturally, mama bear didn't take kindly to this, so she went after the dog and chased it back into the crowd. Generally speaking, being pursued by a 1,000-pound angry bear would be enough for most dogs to take the hint, but this particular pit bull was persistent—or particularly dim—and needed to be chased back into the crowd several times before it got the hint.

Now, let's not overlook the relevant phrase here: "chased back into the crowd." Yes, this dog caused a rather unfortunate interaction between bear and terrified onlookers. The same people who were *ooh*ing and *aah*ing at baby bear's cuddly cuteness a few minutes prior were now running and screaming at the top of their lungs from a very large, very ticked-off mammal bent on defending its young. Mama bear was finally scared away after some quick thinker hurled a camcorder at her. A *Maryville Daily Times* reporter dryly noted, "The camcorder did not survive the ordeal."

Fortunately, no living thing was seriously injured in the dog's attack on the cub, the bear's attack on the dog, or the camcorder's attack on the bear. However, the dog sustained minor injuries consistent with a bear attack, and that along with eyewitness accounts of Stanley's pickup were enough to help rangers track Stanley down and cite him for harassing wildlife, having an unsecured pet, and creating a hazardous situation. Each of these charges is worth a maximum of $5,000 in fines and/or six months in the clink.

A New Leash on Life
All of which could have been avoided if Stanley had followed the rules and kept his dog restrained. But that's all right. He might have 18 months in his own personal kennel to think it over.

Sources: *Maryville Daily Times*, *Knoxville News-Sentinel*, Great Smoky Mountains National Park Resource Management and Science Weekly Update

A FISHY PREMISE

Kids usually learn early on that the world of animation does not accurately reflect life. This typically happens at about age five, when they leap off something high and discover to their surprise that running very quickly will *not* actually allow them to wade in the air for the several crucial seconds required to get back on the ledge. (Learning experiences such as these are typically accompanied by quick visits to the emergency room, followed by ice cream for the kids and Valium for the parents.)

Be that as it may, every so often adults feel the need to step in and remind the tots that just because cuddly animated creatures are doing something doesn't mean it's a good idea in the real world. Such was the impetus for the June 2003 press release issued by JWC Environmental Inc., a Costa Mesa, CA, company that manufactures sewage treatment machinery, and put out in the wake (no pun intended) of the feel-good Pixar-Disney animated film *Finding Nemo*.

Nemo Meets the Muffin Monster

The makers of the "Muffin Monster" waste shredder were concerned that children might replicate a particular incident in the film, and so sought to dissuade them with a press release that would give Hieronymus Bosch the cold shakes:

"In this summer's blockbuster family film *Finding Nemo*, a fish tries a daring escape from an aquarium by jumping down a sink drain, flowing through the city sewer system and out into the open ocean," the press release read. "While it's a touching story, the reality is many sewage treatment plants have large, powerful Muffin Monster grinders that shred solids into tiny particles. In truth, no one would ever find Nemo and the movie would be called 'Grinding Nemo.'"

For those readers who were not immediately sidetracked by the mental image of the adorable baby clown fish of the film graphically chummed down to scale fragments and effluvia, the press release goes on to describe its company's machines in chilling detail: huge grinders reaching seven and a half feet in height, with two massive, counterrotating shafts whose blades overlap, like pinking shears, and which are "powerful enough to shred anything that finds its way into the waste water channel, including clothing, shoes, sticks, rocks, and even car keys."

Should Nemo or any other creature somehow escape the whirring blades of such sewage processing, never fear. "The tertiary process in a plant usually consists of chlorination or UV disinfection," the release assures us, "which kills any remaining organisms."

Is This the End of Nemo?

Let us pause for a moment to recognize the fact that the hellish instruments described in the press release serve a legitimate and useful purpose, helping humanity separate out its junk so that our oceans don't have to receive any more car fenders or detergent boxes than it already does. Chopping up solid refuse allows for easier chemical treatment and helps the organic portions of the waste, like table scraps, decompose (the inorganic portions settle out in a section of the treatment plant called the "grit room" and are ultimately shipped to a landfill). Despite the horrific end these machines promise to any live creature flushed down the pipes, the alternative to dumping raw sewage into the oceans is not a good one. Also, of course, dropping live animals into your pipes is just plain mean and should be avoided, so credit to the press release on that score.

Then Why Did They Name It Muffin Monster?
Still—promoting one's sewage treatment products by warning people how effectively they would grind up a computer-generated fish designed for children to identify with is more than a little weird and macabre. And woe to the parent who takes what he or she learns in this press release and shares it with little Timmy and Claire. For kids just getting over the fact that they can't actually hover in midair, ground-up fishies are just a greased downhill path to therapy.

Sources: Associated Press, JWC Environmental Inc.

* * *

"When a stupid man is doing something he is ashamed of, he always declares that it is his duty."
—**George Bernard Shaw**

DUMB MOVIE FESTIVAL: *SWEPT AWAY* (2002)

Our Entry: *Swept Away*, starring Madonna and Adriano Giannini

The Plot (Such As It Is): In this remake of a controversial 1974 film by Lina Wertmuller, Madonna plays a rich, spoiled woman who is shipwrecked with a sailor (Giannini) whom she had belittled and abused. Soon, he slaps her around and makes her bring him food, and she likes it, which is somehow not surprising.

Directed by Madonna's husband, Guy Ritchie, which is notable in that someone funded the film despite the awful critical and financial reception of the last film Madonna did with her husband, 1985's *Shanghai Surprise* (with ex-husband Sean Penn), not to mention the critical and financial reception of Madonna films in general.

Fun Fact: Giannini's father, Giancarlo Giannini, played the same role in the 1974 version of the film. He was better. It was better.

Total North American Box Office: $598,645 (source: The-Numbers.com). That's right, it made less than a million dollars.

The Critics Rave!

"*Swept Away* is a deserted island movie during which I desperately wished the characters had chosen one movie to take along if they were stranded on a deserted island, and were showing it to us instead of this one."—*Chicago Sun-Times*

"One of the many thoughts that go through your mind while watching *Swept Away* is how hellish life will be in the Guy Ritchie household from now on. After all, it's hard to imagine another director ever making his wife look so bad in a major movie."—*Arizona Republic*

"The biggest husband-and-wife disaster since John and Bo Derek made the ridiculous *Bolero* . . . Writer-director Guy Ritchie shows none of the flair he displayed in *Snatch*; opting instead for lousy gags, clumsy editing, and a wildly careening tone . . . Madonna reads her lines as if she were in a high-school poetry class being taught what syllables to stress: 'Where would we all BE if we all DID things when we FELT like it?'"—Reel.com

"When Madonna and Ritchie wed, I prayed their union would not produce a movie like *Swept Away*. Sometimes prayers don't come true."—*Northwest Herald* (Crystal Lake, IL)

"There's no novelty, no shock value, in watching Madonna being slapped around by Giannini and humiliated into submission . . . After watching her crawl around on all fours and being chained to her lover's bed in the video for 'Express Yourself,' the sight of Madonna kissing Giannini's feet and calling him 'master' just feels like more of the same-old."—*Miami Herald*

"*Swept Away* accomplishes the impossible: It makes you feel sorry for Madonna."—*Washington Post*

THIS RESCUE WAS ALL WET

The boy told the rescue team who plucked him off the cliff that he was afraid his new shoes would get wet. Which is slightly confusing, because if the boy wanted to make sure his shoes stayed dry, climbing on rocks on the English shore with five other friends was surely a funny way to do it—especially since the six of them wandered off so far that they were cut off by the tides and required rescuing.

The other five boys were easily rescued by lifeboats. But our Boy Whose Shoes Must Stay Dry was too clever for that. Rather than risk dampening his shoes, he climbed up a cliff—and got stuck. He had to be extracted through the use of a chopper, an air-sea rescue drama that cost in the area of $40,000. The cost of the shoes, which, apparently, did stay dry: about $110.

The shoes, interestingly enough, were Rockports. We'd like to note that Rockports are generally known for their water resistance. A bit of sales fluff for the Rockport Canyon Vista APM31001 Outdoor Performance Shoe: "The Rockport® Canyon Vista outdoor shoe for men is seam-sealed waterproof for durability."

So you can see why keeping these shoes dry was absolutely imperative.

Source: *Sun* (U.K.)

A DOG DAY AFTERNOON

For some people, it's not enough that they hate dogs and don't want any as pets. They also hate your dog and don't want you to have any either. "Jurgen," from Harrislee, Germany, was one of those people. We don't know why he hated his neighbor's German shepherd so much, but he did.

And one day, he decided to do something about it. He called the police and complained that the dog was disturbing the peace with his barking. The police notified Jurgen's dog-owning neighbor of the complaint.

The neighbor thought there was something fishy about the complaint. So when he went out to his yard to investigate, he found, in the hedge . . . a speaker which was attached to a cable leading back to Jurgen's house.

This time the police to payed a call to Jurgen the Doghater. They turned on the sound system and the speaker started making barking and clicking sounds —just the sort of noises that get a dog all riled up. Apparently the German shepherd in question wasn't making nearly enough noise for Jurgen to complain about, so Jurgen gave the dog a little encouragement.

And there you have it—a clear-cut case of canine entrapment. "The whole story is so ludicrous, we really can't imagine what he thought he would achieve," a police spokesmen told reporters.

It sounds like Jurgen could use a hug. Or maybe a nice puppy.

Source: Reuters

TIPS FOR STUPID CRIMINALS

We've learned everything we know from episodes of
Law & Order: Criminal Intent!

AS DUMB AS WATCHING PAINT DRY
Today's tip: Pick up after yourself.

Our crook, "Brandon," got it in his mind to rob a house. In the process of committing his felonious activity, he tipped over a bucket of paint in the garage of the home he was burgling. Then, in a rush to head off with his ill-gotten goods, Brandon forgot to check his feet.

The police were not so careless; they noticed that someone had gotten paint on his shoes and was leaving a trail of footprints. They tracked the footprints to a hotel, where they found Brandon, a pair of paint-caked shoes, and presumably a very bad alibi. Off to the slammer for Brandon, presumably without his shoes.

Source: Associated Press

* * *

"Those who realize their folly are not true fools."
—Chuang-tzu

NO GOOD DEED GOES UNPUNISHED

Members of the county council in Staffordshire, England, were each given £10,000 (about $16,000) to spend on "good causes." Being the sort of book this is, you might expect us to tell you they spent it on strip clubs and dinners with friends, but no.

Staffordshire county councillor Robert Marshall allocated a portion of his share to purchase one of those speed cameras. You know, the ones that snap a picture of your car as you blast through an intersection and then nail you for bad driving even when there is no human being around to catch you. Isn't technology wonderful?

Paybacks Are Hell

Councillor Marshall found out just how wonderful it is as he zipped through a 30-mph area at 42 mph and got a ticket courtesy of the very same camera his allocation had purchased. The ticket took him up to six points on his record (12 short of a suspended license but nothing his insurance company is going to be thrilled about). You would think, having given the camera to the county, that he might have asked where they intended to place it.

Like any good politician, Marshall positioned this personal defeat as a moral victory. "My experience proves that the cameras are totally indiscriminate and that they are working." What a spin job! Still, we bet that with next year's "good deeds" money, he buys something safe and non-ticket-producing.

Source: BBC

TURN ON YOUR ART LIGHT

When the Scottish repairman looked up at a flickering lightbulb on a street sign in Glasgow on a July day in 2003, he thought to himself: "This needs to be fixed. And I need to fix it." So he did, and it was done, and our repairman moved on, happy in the knowledge that he had fulfilled his destiny. Hey, he's a repairman. He repairs.

Little did our repairman know that the lightbulb he fixed was *supposed* to be blinking. It was a critical element of a massive, $300,000 art installation, designed by Douglas Gordon, a winner of the prestigious Turner Prize (a sort of Nobel prize for the artsy set). The flickering lightbulb was supposed to replicate a similarly flickering bulb in Alfred Hitchcock's 1958 film *Vertigo*.

When informed of the fixed-but-yet-did-not-need-fixing bulb, the Glasgow City Council indignantly proclaimed that none of their repairmen fixed the street sign. But consider this: The street sign, and the installation it was a part of, had been up since 1998. It took five years for someone to get around to "fixing" that lightbulb. That has *all* the hallmarks of government efficiency.

In case you're wondering, the "repaired" sign will be returned to its former, flickering self by the Glasgow Visual Arts Project. Expect it to be "fixed" again sometime in late 2008.

Sources: *Daily Mail*, Ananova

GOLDEN RULE DAYS

It's important to teach children manners. At Hu Zhuang Elementary School in Beijing, the educators decided to back up their etiquette lessons with financial penalties. In addition to new rules that forbid littering or coughing without covering the mouth, Hu Zhuang now forbids passing gas. Anyone who gets caught having a methane moment is fined the equivalent of 75 cents.

The decision was immediately controversial. "To form good habits is important," a teacher named Gao told *Sina News*. "But according to Department of Education regulations, schools have no right to fine."

In addition, how do you go about enforcing such a rule? The intestinal functions of schoolchildren are highly, shall we say, dynamic. Even the best-behaved kids are at the mercy of whatever their parents fed them for breakfast. Plus, the system is ripe for abuse; if the school is ever short on funds, the administration could make the cafeteria serve beans five days running.

Another teacher noted that since the rule was implemented, no child had been fined. That doesn't mean that the gassing has stopped. It just means that the children might have quickly become masters of the "silent but deadly" technique, which we suppose is marginally more polite than your usual violent outburst, but probably not what the rulemakers had intended. In any event, you can't say that the kids at Hu Zhuang Elementary aren't learning new things.

Sources: *Sina News*, Ananova

SHE SCREAMED FOR ICE CREAM

Everybody loves ice cream. Most people also know that if you eat too much ice cream too fast you will be seized by the dreaded "ice cream brain freeze," which feels as if tiny little demons are congregating at the spot just behind your uvula, and stabbing needle-thin icicles directly into your brain, giggling maniacally and all the while singing jaunty Oompa Loompa–like songs. After a few headaches, you learn how to pace your consumption of ice cream. It's a food that teaches you to eat it daintily.

We assume that "Shen," a 23-year-old woman from Guangzhou, China, had never had a brain freeze. This would explain why one day, Shen came home, opened her refrigerator, grabbed the ice cream, and began to consume it at a frightening rate—so fast that the ice cream demons were unable to get a foothold in the back of her throat. That's good, right?

Think again.

Hold the Cone!

The next day Shen went to the doctor and complained about pain in her throat and stomach. The doctor took a look inside and immediately sent her to the hospital, where she stayed for a week. Shen had eaten so much ice cream so quickly that she had frozen her esophagus. So the next time you experience brain freeze, thank the ice cream demons for saving you from the emergency room.

Sources: *China Daily*, Ananova

HISTORICAL DUMBOSITY: LOUIS XVI'S MONEY PROBLEMS

W e can all agree that when you're a king, a revolution can be dreadfully inconvenient. One day you're minding your own business, running a country and being fanned by courtiers, and the next day, some badly dressed rabble is showing up at the door, talking nonsense about "rights" and "democracy" and asking for your head in a basket. It's scandalous, really. They could at least put on a cravat before asking a person to hand over the country.

For all that, it doesn't pay to underestimate the intelligence of the rabble, or their ability to recognize you while you're fleeing the country. Louis XVI of France found this out in 1791—that's after that whole French Revolution thing you might have heard about— when he, his wife, Marie, and their kids decided that it might be prudent to skip out of Paris and head to Belgium, because the Belgians, for whatever their other shortcomings, wouldn't try to kill them. So Louis and the family disguised themselves as a middle-class merchant family (horrors!) and headed north.

The Not-So-Great Escape

Apparently, they got lost. Louis, demonstrating a take-charge attitude that one usually admires in a king, decided to ask someone for directions. This was despite the urgings of his servants to stay hidden—he was, after all, fleeing the country. Louis must have thought his disguise was *that* good. And maybe it was. But maybe one of Louis's servants shouldn't have thanked the guy who gave them directions by handing him a tip.

A bit of important advice: when fleeing the country in fear for your life, *do not give over a wad of cash that has your face on it.* The French currency of the time featured Louis's mug, and it was a close enough likeness that the guy who gave the directions recognized the "middle-class merchant" as the guy on his cash. He ran to the town hall and announced his discovery. A posse was quickly formed, and Louis and company were apprehended up the road and returned to Paris, where in 1792 Louis was stripped of his crown, and in 1793, stripped of his head.

Now you know why guys don't ask for directions.

* * *

"You can be sincere and still be stupid."
—**Charles F. Kettering**

"Foolproof systems don't take into account the ingenuity of fools."
—**Gene Brown**

"I am afraid only of people who cannot think."
—**Winston Churchill**

TIPS FOR STUPID CRIMINALS

What? You want them to get tips from other stupid criminals?

NO LICENSE TO DRIVE
Today's tip: In fact, the police can arrest
you anywhere.

Our gal "Sal" was driving her car without a
license plate. Naturally, that's a no-no, so when
the fine officers of the Alexandria, Louisiana,
police department saw her drive by, they signaled for
her to pull over. She did not—what she did was speed
up and get on the highway. Soon Sally was zooming
along at nearly a hundred miles an hour, trailing cops
from state, county, *and* local districts behind her.

Where was Sally going? She was going home. With
the cops still behind her, she parked in her driveway
and got out of her car like nothing had happened. You
see, Sally was working under an interesting assumption:
she thought that if the cops were chasing you, and you
made it your own house, they couldn't arrest you—that
you were, quite literally, home free. Sally got this idea,
apparently, from a TV show.

So imagine Sally's surprise when she learned that
you can be arrested at home—and she was, in fact, on
charges including speeding, reckless driving, and failure
to give way to an emergency vehicle. That's what you
get for taking legal advice from your television.

Sources: *Town Talk* (Alexandria, LA), Ananova

TAKING A YEN FOR
PACHINKO A LITTLE TOO FAR

At 6:30 p.m., May 26, 2003, in a pachinko parlor in the Akita prefecture of northern Japan,
deputy governor Takashi Chiba was relaxing
by sending little metal balls through the myriad metal
posts of Japan's favorite vertical pinball machines. And
why not? He'd had a rough day doing . . . well, whatever it was that deputy governors of Japanese prefec-
tures do. But on this particular day Chiba was slightly
more important than most deputy governors. The
actual governor of the Akita prefecture was in South
Korea on a business trip, making Chiba the effective
leader of 1.1 million Akita prefecture citizens.

Well, maybe not the *effective* leader. Because on
that day, at the time Chiba was winging balls through
posts, the Akita prefecture was rocked by a 7.0 earth-
quake that was felt as far south as Tokyo. The temblor
was as strong as the infamous Kobe quake in 1995,
which killed thousands. Fortunately, this time the
epicenter of the quake was offshore, minimizing the
impact on dry land. But when all was said and done
more than 100 Japanese were injured, and damage to
buildings and roads was widespread.

Life Must Go on—Ka-ching!
Faced with a crisis of this magnitude, deputy (acting)
governor Takashi Chiba called upon years of bureau-
cratic experience, plundered the depths of his feelings
about serving his constituency and . . . continued to

play pachinko. And kept on playing. And then, just when you thought he was done, he played some *more*. All told, he played for 45 minutes after the quake. It was more than an hour before he even bothered to contact other prefecture officials to see if anyone was buried under a collapsed highway or something.

Needless to say, by Friday, deputy governor Chiba was out of a job, resigning rather than performing the ritual suicide that would have been expected of him several centuries earlier. Chiba explained to the Kyodo news agency, "I am extremely tired both mentally and physically and have lost confidence in my ability to do my job." He wasn't the only one.

You know what would pick him right up? A nice game of pachinko.

Sources: Reuters, Associated Press

* * *

"Only two things are infinite, the universe and human stupidity, and I'm not sure about the former."
—Albert Einstein

"Idiot, n. A member of a large and powerful tribe whose influence in human affairs has always been dominant and controlling."
—Ambrose Bierce, ***The Devil's Dictionary***

SHE POPPED THE CLUTCH. HE PUT IT INTO GEAR. HEH HEH HEH.

Here's an interesting fact: in Germany, it is legal to have sex while driving a car zooming down the autobahn. Just don't hit anything.

So discovered "Rolf," a 23-year-old Cologne motorist. In June 2003, Rolf picked up a blond hitch-hiker while he was tooling around in his car. The two then decided it might be fun to—ahem—get into gear. Long story short, she got naked and climbed into the driver's seat while Rolf was in it. Rolf, understandably distracted, drove off the pavement and hit a road sign. Let us pause here to consider the comical image of the air bags going off in this little crack-up.

Then Rolf made a big mistake: he drove off in a hurry. This was a no-no, because although having sex while operating a moving vehicle is not a crime in Germany, racing away from damage you've created is. Rolf was tracked down by the police and hauled into court. There he was convicted of a hit-and-run and fined 600 euros (about $600). He also had to pay for the sign he mowed down in his moment of vehicular passion. That was another 400 euros. Hope it was worth it.

Why isn't having sex while driving a car illegal in Germany? Said court spokesman Juergen Mannebeck: "It's a situation lawmakers never thought about."

Source: Reuters

TIPS FOR STUPID CRIMINALS

Why? Because we're not going to pay their bail.

I'VE POSITIVELY ID'D MYSELF
Today's tip: Try not to leave behind massive amounts of evidence.

Poor "Brad" wanted a cell phone. But Brad didn't want to pay for it. This fundamental dissonance between desire and stinginess is probably what caused Brad to bolt from a Chino Hills, California, Radio Shack with a cell phone in hand but without paying for it.

Brad's five-fingered cellular discount might have worked too, if not for two basic flaws in Brad's mode of thievery. First, while casing the joint, he cleverly disguised his criminal intent by posing as a customer, filling out a credit application. Not so cleverly, however, he used his real name and address on the application, which made it nice and easy for the cops to track him down later.

Second, while admiring all the nifty functions of the cell phone he would subsequently snatch from the store, Brad took a picture of himself with the cell phone's built-in digital camera—a picture that was then stored on a computer in the store. This allowed a member of the store's staff to make a positive ID of Brad by comparing the cell phone picture with Brad's driver's license photo.

Dial "D" for Dumb.

Source: Associated Press

IS THAT A BOMB IN YOUR SHOE, OR ARE YOU JUST HAPPY TO SEE ME?

There are certain classes of people we expect to say stupid things to airport security people.

They are, in no particular order: hostile teens, professional-but-not-successful comedians, conspiracy theorists, anarchists, very important people who think the rules couldn't *possibly* apply to them, the paranoid, the permanently aggrieved, and people who were once married to airport security people. And, of course, actual criminals carrying drugs and/or explosives in their bags. Let's not forget about them.

One group that we *don't* expect to crack jokes to the security folks are actual, honest-to-goodness pilots. So imagine our surprise when "Pierre," a copilot for an Air France flight from JFK airport to Paris allegedly attempted some comedy stylings to amuse the security detail.

Lost in Translation

Pierre was going through the security checkpoint when he balked at removing his shoes. The details at this point are sketchy. Some people report that Pierre actually said, "I have a bomb in my shoe"—bringing to mind airline passenger Richard Reid, who in December 2001 tried to light a bomb he'd hidden in his shoe—while others report he said, in a sarcastic tone, "Well, what do you think, I have a bomb on me?"

If it was a joke, it bombed. You know those security people—they're a tough audience. Not to mention the fact that New York City security people are the *most* unlikely crowd to find a joke like that amusing. Pierre was quickly arrested by the New York Port Authority police.

Instead of flying through the air with the greatest of ease, Pierre's flight was canceled (it was missing a copilot, after all), and 353 passengers who were hoping to get to Paris instead spent another night in the Big Apple. Pierre was charged with falsely reporting a threat in the first and second degrees, which carries a maximum sentence of seven years in the Big House. It just goes to show: it's always the people that you least expect.

Sources: *New York Times*, Associated Press

* * *

THEY'RE COMING

English drivers were so distracted by a pair of giant inflatable space aliens that the M1 roadway in Derbyshire snarled into a four-mile traffic jam that caused two small accidents. Police suspect the aliens, each 27 feet high, were inflated to mark the anniversary of the 1947 "Roswell Incident," in which an alien craft is alleged to have crashed in New Mexico (but did not cause a four-mile traffic jam—the aliens were more considerate back then).

Source: *Evening Standard*

THE REALLY STUPID QUIZ: SENSITIVITY

Once again, we've come to another edition of the Really Stupid Quiz! Pick out which of the following "news stories" is actually true. Does your answer say something about you? Maybe.

1. An office supplies vendor had his contract with the city of Berkeley, California, yanked after he allegedly violated the city's discrimination laws by comparing city employees to cows. The complaint, filed by a worker in the city's public works department, alleges that the vendor joked loudly that the office was filled with "the bovine, awaiting slaughter," which the worker took to be a comment on both the largely female staff and the weight of some of its members, thereby showing discrimination based on sex and physical characteristics.

"All I said was I was glad I had a job that let me get out and move around, instead of being penned up like a veal in an office all day," said the vendor. "I didn't say anything about anybody else but me." The vendor is now appealing and is considering suing the city for violating his contract.

2. New Zealand farmers struck back at a government spokesperson who derided a protest by farmers as "an example of what happens when you get too close to your sheep." New Zealand farmers had been participating in a "Raise a Stink" campaign to protest a "flat-

ulence tax" levied against sheep and cows to combat global warming. In the protest, farmers mailed manure to government officials. This prompted the comment by a spokesperson for New Zealand's agricultural ministry; the spokesperson later maintained the comment was meant to be off the record.

More than 30 Kiwi farmers responded to the comment by dumping wheelbarrows full of sheep poop on the steps of the ministry and demanding an apology and the resignation of the spokesperson. The farmers were arrested but later released. The spokesperson did indeed apologize and was placed on leave pending an internal investigation.

3. Blonde jokes are incredibly popular in Bosnia, but not for much longer: a new law, set to go into effect, will make it illegal to tell blonde jokes. It's part of a new gender equity law, which, as one human rights official tells it, "would enable blonde women to sue anyone who tells jokes that offend them, even if those jokes were just based on the color of their hair." Presumably the law would also cover jokes made about women whose hair is any other color as well.

Which one is really stupid?

Answer page 311.

Sources: Ananova, *Nezavisne Novine*

DUMB MOVIE FESTIVAL: BALLISTIC: ECKS VS. SEVER (2002)

Our Entry: *Ballistic: Ecks vs. Sever*, starring Antonio Banderas and Lucy Liu

The Plot (Such As It Is): Lucy Liu is an American secret agent who has gone off the rails; the United States, apparently short of agents, brings in retired agent Antonio Banderas to track her down.

Many deaths and explosions follow, and then there's something about miniature assassination tools, followed by deaths and explosions, and then something about small children in danger, after which follow more deaths and explosions. No one has really been able to figure out what's going on in this film, except for the deaths and explosions.

Fun Fact: It is based on a video game, and not even a very popular or good one. Also, the director's nickname is Kaos, which should have been a warning rather than a recommendation.

Total North American Box Office: $14,294,842 (source: The-Numbers.com). That's off a $70 million budget.

The Critics Rave!

"The picture looks as if it were lighted with a 20-watt bulb. And it is dim in more ways than one."—*New York Times*

"I'm guessing the director (who simply goes by the moniker Kaos—how funny is that?) is a magician. After all, he took three minutes of dialogue [and] 30 seconds of plot and turned them into a 90-minute movie that feels five hours long."
—*Arizona Republic*

"For years, people have joked about an action movie that might eliminate plot altogether and simply cut to the pyrotechnics. Someone has finally done it."—*USA Today*

"All the emotional depth of a video game, and the dramatic coherence we associate with the lesser works of Ed Wood."
—*MountainX.com*

"So fraught with howlingly bad dialogue and seizure-inducing action that it almost made me wish for the relative tranquility and incisive screenwriting of *Pokémon*."
—*The Republican* (Oakland, MD)

"A picture for idiots."—*Seattle Times*

"The movie stars Lucy Liu as Sever, a former agent for the Defense Intelligence Agency, [and] Antonio Banderas is Ecks, a former ace FBI agent who is coaxed back into service . . . both of these U.S. agencies wage what amounts to warfare in Vancouver, which is actually in a nation named Canada, which has agencies and bureaus of its own and takes a dim view of machineguns, rocket launchers, plastic explosives and the other weapons the American agents and their enemies use to litter the streets of the city with the dead."—*Chicago Sun-Times*

IT WAS JUST LIKE THE LOVE BOAT, EXCEPT FOR THOSE DARN FEDERAL AGENTS

Most people dream of taking a leisurely cruise through warm climes. But most people are not "Cindy," a 20-year-old passenger on the Royal Caribbean ship *Legend of the Seas*. It was late April 2003 and Cindy was not rejoicing in *Legend of the Seas*'s ample entertainment options. The Anchors Aweigh Lounge offered live music and dancing! The That's Entertainment theater was performing vaudeville on the high seas! And let's not forget the chance to eat until you drop: buffets, buffets, buffets! We aren't sure why Cindy took the cruise in the first place, since she was more interested in getting back to her boyfriend in Orange County, California. She probably realized it would be kind of difficult to get the other 2,400 or so passengers and crew to cut their cruises short just so *she* could get back to her man. But Cindy was resourceful. She had a plan—to plant fake terrorist notes on the ship. That way, the ship would have no choice but to turn around and go home.

Not Only Brilliant, But Foolproof

And it would have worked, too, if it weren't for those meddling Feds. Rather than turn the ship around, they routed it to a location off the island of Oahu, Hawaii— pretty much opposite the direction Cindy wanted to go—and greeted it with a contingent of FBI agents, who thoroughly checked the ship for biological, chemical, radiological, and explosive weapons, and interrogated the ship's passengers and crew.

So, rather than getting home to spend snuggle time with her honeykins, as was her intention, Cindy found herself placed in front of U.S. Magistrate Judge Kevin Chang, who charged her with two counts of violating title 18, United States Code, Sections 2332b (a)(2) and 2332b (a)(1)(A), "Acts of terrorism transcending national boundaries." She began a two-year prison term in November.

You're on Your Own Kid

Cindy's mother told the *Los Angeles Times*, "She is going to have to stay in jail and learn her lesson. This was a big, big problem, and if she has to sit in jail—oh well. She's going to have to deal with it."

Interestingly, it was later reported that Cindy's boyfriend—the man for whom she did jail time—had earlier done a 90-day stint in the Orange County Jail. So now they have a common experience! That'll just bring them even *closer* together. Although for their honeymoon, maybe they should just skip the cruise.

Sources: Associated Press, *Los Angeles Times*, OC Weekly (Costa Mesa, CA), Federal Bureau of Investigation

* * *

"If stupidity got us into this mess, then why can't it get us out?"

—Will Rogers

SEE YOU LATER ALLIGATOR

When Michael McCormick saw a five-foot-long alligator heading toward a woman and her four children near an elementary school in Tavares, Florida, he didn't think twice about what he should do. McCormick got out of his truck, caught the alligator with a loop of rope, and secured the animal to a chain-link fence. He then asked a friend to call the police while he made sure the animal didn't get away.

The police came and contacted Florida's Fish and Wildlife Conservation Commission, who fined McCormick $180 for possessing an alligator. Dumb as this ticket was, the rationale was a good one: "People can't be taking this in their own hands. We're just going to end up with more people getting bitten and injured," a spokesperson told the *Orlando Sentinel*.

Remember, just because you think you can handle a live alligator doesn't mean you can. In this case, however, ticketing McCormick seems sort of dim. The Fish and Wildlife spokesperson suggested that McCormick should have focused his efforts on moving the woman and her children. But *you* try getting four kids to move in the same direction at one time. Roping the gator was almost certainly the more time-efficient move. Interestingly, after McCormick roped the alligator, the police had him release it into a nearby pond, where the Fish and Wildlife team set meat-filled traps to recapture it. A day later, the traps were still gator-free. Watch your step down there in Tavares, folks.

Source: *Orlando Sentinel*

YOUR CAT IS IN FOR A SHOCK

What happens when you don't pay your electricity bill? Well, in most places your electricity would be shut off. Then you sit in the dark like your ancestors, until that big glowing ball in the sky comes up again and you do the hunter-gatherer thing with your cavemates. Since we're more conditioned to watch TV than to hunt woolly mammoths, switching off the electricity is enough to get our attention.

But not in Vladivostok, Russia, where electricity company Dalenergo is owed hundreds of millions of rubles by recalcitrant customers. Cutting off the electricity just isn't cutting it—despite the lack of juice for TVs, toasters, and lighting fixtures, thousands of customers are refusing to pay up.

So Dalenergo has decided to take another tack: director Nikolai Tkachyov told Russian television that it was planning to confiscate customers' pets until said customers coughed up the cash. "Let the father answer his daughter's question as to why her favorite cat has been taken away," Tkachyov reportedly said.

The suggestion that public utility might put its customers' pets in hock raised such a stink that Dalenergo's owner, Unified Energy System, felt the need to rush out a press release to assure Vladivostok citizens that Fidovich and Fluffanya would be safe. "Dalenergo will not take away Vladivostok residents' four-footed friends," the release read. Of course, that still leaves birds and fish at risk. Better pay the bill, just to be sure.

Source: Reuters

THE RUNNING
OF THE MORONS

Running with the bulls in Pamplona: dumb. The bulls are run down the street to a bull ring, in which they will all soon be killed. No matter what, those bulls are doomed. Inasmuch as this is the case, these animals are entirely within their rights to take out as many humans as possible before they get to their destination, as a way to even out the karmic scales.

What sort of person would place himself in front of a ton of angry, confused animals just for the fun of it? Running in front of a rampaging bull to save a child? Fine—admirable, even. Running in front of a rampaging bull to save a kitten? That's fine, too. Running in front of a rampaging bull for your own amusement? You're a damned fool.

A Lot of Bulls

Just about the only thing the running of the bulls has going for it is tradition: they've been doing it for centuries, and you know how they are about tradition in Europe. If they've been doing it since forever, then that's a good enough reason to keep doing it. The major drawback is that Pamplona is in Spain, which as we all know is far away from North America, where a remarkable number of dumb guys would happily taunt a bull.

Now there is good news for dumb North Americans: you don't have to go to Spain to be trampled by bulls. In Strathmore, Alberta, Canada, there's a new attraction for the Town's Heritage Days: the Heritage Days Stampede. In the stampede, up to 30 bulls chase a couple hundred Canadians and Americans who have paid $100 Canadian for the privilege. Should they survive (the runners, not the bulls), they get a T-shirt and a bandanna. "It's guaranteed adrenaline," organizer Jim Cammeart told the *Ottawa Citizen* newspaper.

This Idea Is Bull***!

And now, a comment from the loyal opposition: Dr. Louis Francescutti, director of the Edmonton-based Alberta Centre for Injury and Control Research. "I think this would rank up there as the most idiotic idea I have heard in my life," the doctor told the *Citizen*. "These people really need to get their heads checked."

We're with the good doctor on this one, although we'd like to point out that this won't stop a bunch of sensation junkies from seeing if they can outrace steers. We just hope they'll remember when they get a hoof through the spleen that they don't even have the excuse that this is something people having been doing since the Middle Ages. This is all-new stupidity.

Enjoy it, guys.

Source: *Ottawa Citizen*

* * *

"The easiest person to deceive is oneself."
—**Edward Bluwer-Lytton**

TIPS FOR STUPID CRIMINALS

Ensuring a better grade of stupid criminal for your future!

IT TAKES A THIEF
Today's tip: Make the effort, pal.

Look, if you're going to steal something, at least show some *initiative*. Even a basic "slip under the shirt" maneuver shows that you understand you're breaking the law and that you know you're doing something the public frowns upon. The rest of us appreciate that glimmer of shame, you know?

"Chuck" skipped this chapter of the "How to Steal" handbook, and it showed when he entered the Palm Bay, Florida, Wal-Mart with the intention of snagging himself a computer. Allegedly, Chuck simply went up to a computer display at the store, picked up a computer that looked good to him and then headed toward the exit. Naturally, he was stopped by the store loss-prevention officer. Chuck, apparently shocked that his thievery was so easily discerned, got in a scuffle with the officer and at one point even bit his thumb. Chuck was eventually subdued and charged with grand theft, retail theft, and aggravated battery.

We're not saying that Chuck would have gotten away with stuffing the computer under his shirt (that'd be a pretty loose shirt, for one thing). But at least then we could give him some credit for the attempt. As it is, Chuck gets a big fat zero. Better luck next time, Chuck!

Source: Local6.com

THE REALLY STUPID QUIZ: THOSE CRAZY TEENS!

Would you look at that? Here it is, time for another Really Stupid Quiz! Guess which of these scenarios really happened in the real world.

1. A German teen's parents went away, so of course he had one of those parties, with a destructive intensity you usually only get in Hollywood teen films. Realizing that he didn't have enough time to clean up before his parents got home, our teen decided on an alternate strategy: he called the police and claimed that robbers had ransacked the house. One minor issue with the story: nothing was actually stolen. The police began putting the squeeze on the kid, who admitted he was covering up. They charged him with wasting police time *and* they told his parents. The rats!

2. Three Manchester, New Hampshire, teens decided they'd gotten enough flak from one of their teachers, who had recently given the three of them a poor grade on a history project. So they decided to get back at him. They captured a squirrel, which they placed in their teacher's desk before class. During class, the teacher heard the animal moving around in the desk and opened the drawer it was in; the terrified squirrel launched itself at the teacher and bit him on the chin before escaping through an open window. The teacher, reeling from the pain, accidentally struck his head on the classroom door and collapsed, uncon-

scious, dislocating the ring and pinky fingers of his left hand as the weight of his body fell on them. The squirrel was never found, and the teacher had to get a preventative rabies vaccination at the hospital. One of the teens confessed; all three were eventually charged with assault and suspended from school. Extra credit is not an option.

3. The latest craze among Japanese schoolgirls: ultraviolet tattoos. Japanese newspaper *Asahi Shimbun* reported on a new ultraviolet ink that allows people to place temporary tattoos on their skin that are all but invisible in normal light and glow vibrantly when exposed to black lights—like those in clubs. "It's the best of both worlds," one schoolgirl said. "I can express my individuality while at the same time being modest and practical during the day."

Popular tattoos include Bugs Bunny and characters from the *Love, Hina* anime series. One drawback is that the ink causes a severe allergic rash in about 5 percent of the girls who use it; in one case a Tokyo teen was sent to the hospital for treatment. Legislators are now considering a ban on the temporary tattoos but admit that short of installing black lights at schools, it may not be possible to see who is wearing them and who is not.

Which one is really stupid?

Answer page 311.

Source: Ananova

A GUN IN THE OVEN

S o, you have a handgun. If you're not using it you need to store it in a safe and secure place.

Do you:

a) Take ammunition out of the gun and place it into a lockable gun box, and store it in a safe and secure place
b) Toss that still-loaded weapon into a bag and chuck the bag into an oven

If you're the sort of person to say "choice b looks good to me," you're the sort of person who makes the rest of us *really* nervous, and you need to rethink your firearm storage policies.

Now You're Cooking
"Quentin" had a bag with two handguns that he needed to store. For reasons beyond comprehension, Quentin decided to put them into the oven. So that's what he did and then off he went.

A little while later housemate "Sadie" decided to use the oven. She turned the oven on to preheat it. She didn't check it first to see if there was a bag of guns inside, because really, why would she? So the guns baked, and the bag they were in started to smoke. *That* Sadie noticed. She opened the oven to find out what was in there, which was the cue for one of the guns to go off. *Bang,* a bullet went through her forearm, hip, and thigh.

At the hospital, recovering from her wounds, Sadie tried to convince the staff that she'd been struck by exploding glass from the oven, but those clever medical folk know a gunshot wound when they see one. They called the police, and the police eventually arrested Quentin. He was arraigned on assault and weapons charges and held without bail.

Source: Associated Press

* * *

MORE BURNING STUPIDITY

Two women stealing gas from a small Alaskan town's gas pump nearly paid with their lives when one of them used a lighter to look into the gas tank—while the other woman was still pumping gas. The next thing the two women knew, their clothes were on fire. The two put each other out and then ran away, leaving burning gas on the ground 10 feet from a tank holding 3,000 gallons of gas, and close to a dozen 27,000-gallon tanks of gasoline and fuel oil. Local police put out the flames before everything went ka-pow. The women were charged with criminally negligent burning, reckless endangerment, and fourth-degree theft.

Source: *Anchorage Daily News*

BONO'S HAT TRICK

We have very little bad to say about Bono, lead singer of U2. He's a big rock star and could spend his days in mindless pursuits. Instead, he spends a lot of his time talking to bureaucrats worldwide, trying to get them to forgive third-world debts so those underdeveloped countries might spend a little of their gross national product on something besides interest payments.

Even so, Bono has an occasional lapse. And we're not just talking about the 1997 Pop Mart tour, although we could go on for hours about *that*. No, what we're thinking of at the moment was a day in late May 2003, when the vocalist flew to Italy to take part in a benefit concert with his good friend Luciano Pavarotti.

It seems that once Bono arrived in Pavarotti's hometown of Modena, he realized to his horror that he had left his favorite hat in England. The Grammy-winning musician was bereft; after all, what good is it to sell tens of millions of albums worldwide if you don't have your favorite hat to share it with?

Mr. Hat Only Travels First Class

Big deal, you say. Just have someone mail the damn hat. But no! It was a *special* hat. And thus it began a special journey. A special, *expensive* journey. First the hat was placed in a cab and shuttled from West London to Gatwick Airport. That cost about $160, fare and tip included. Then it was placed on a British

Airways flight to Bologna, Italy. Cargo hold? Not on your life, baby! This hat went first class all the way—to the tune of over $700. Just imagine what the guy sitting next to the hat thought about. He should have asked for the hat's complimentary champagne.

Mr. Hat Gets an Upgrade
And maybe he did—and perhaps even got a little unruly, which may be why the first-class flight attendants decided that first class was not good enough and transported the hat into the cockpit. That's right, the hat got to ride with the captain! After the hat landed, it was taken to Modena by a driver specially hired for the occasion—another $240 or so. Throw in insurance and additional tips, and all together Bono spent more than $1,500 just to get his hat.

It Was All Worth It
A source from Bono's camp noted that the amount he'd spent to get his hat sent was "nothing compared to the amount he'll have raised on the night" of the benefit concert. Maybe not. But for future reference, Bono, two words for you: Federal Express. Maybe it won't make for as colorful a story. But you'll still get your hat.

Sources: London *Sun*, Ananova

* * *

"Whenever a man does a thoroughly stupid thing it is always from the noblest motive."

—Oscar Wilde

DAGNABBIT! THE GAS PEDAL MOVED ON ITS OWN!

At 85, "Harry" may have been considered too old to drive by many people. But Harry was not one of those people; he'd been driving all this time and, by gum, he wanted to keep driving. He was even going to take a driving test at the Van Nuys, California, branch of the Department of Motor Vehicles to prove he still had what it took.

And give Harry this much—he was able to start his engine just fine. But then came the part where he hit that handicapped parking sign. Which was followed by hitting the accelerator pedal instead of the brake pedal. Which was immediately followed by Harry smashing into a building. No one was killed or injured, but Harry's car suffered damage, as did the building he plowed into. And which building was that? Why, the Department of Motor Vehicles, of course. Harry was moving his car in order to get onto the street to take the test.

How Not to Pass Your Driving Test

Alas for Harry—when you crash your car into the DMV while your test instructor is *right there watching you*, it's difficult to argue that you're still competent behind the wheel. Harry's license was revoked pending the investigation of his car accident. Hopefully he had someone to take him home. A bad day for Harry, but a good day for other drivers, not to mention other buildings and handicapped parking signs in Southern California.

Source: NBC4.tv

DUMB MOVIE FESTIVAL: GLITTER (2001)

Our Entry: *Glitter*, starring Mariah Carey and no one else you know

The Plot (Such As It Is): An unassuming singer played by Carey strikes it huge in the early '80s. You may ask yourself, what is Mariah Carey doing playing Whitney Houston? Which is what we were asking when her first album came out. But never mind that. This film is basically a rehash of *A Star Is Born* with a little maternal drama thrown in for good measure. Carey is kept from speaking too much, which is good, but she still manages to utter dialogue on occasion, which is not so good.

Fun Fact: Based on the awful performance of this film and the accompanying soundtrack, Mariah Carey was released from an expensive recording contract with a $28 million buyout. So essentially she got $28 million for making a flop movie and album. How's that for failing upward?

Total North American Box Office: $4,273,372 (source: The-Numbers.com). Small comfort for the studio: it cost $8.5 million to make. The film was released after Carey's highly publicized mental collapse and also just after the 9/11 tragedy, both factored in its underwhelming performance.

The Critics Rave!

"The worst thing about *Glitter* is not that it's sappy . . . The worst thing about the movie is that it's been made by people who aren't even trying. A lot of the biggest head-scratchers in the plotting could have been explained by maybe one quick line of dialogue or one pointed visual indicator. But the filmmakers don't even bother doing that much work."
—Daily-Reviews.com

"You'd have a breakdown, too, if you were stuck in a movie as drab and glum as *Glitter*."—*St. Paul Pioneer Press*

"About as fresh as rancid Chinese food that has been stuck in the back of the refrigerator for several months . . . Life is far too short to waste it on a motion picture as devoid of intelligence and entertainment value as *Glitter*."
—Themovieboy.com

"There is good. There is bad. There is worse and terrible and pathetic and painful. Then there is *Glitter*."
—The Cranky Critic

"[Carey's] inert, glassy-eyed performance is so disastrous she can't even manage to lip synch convincingly."—*Miami Herald*

"If *Glitter* is a cry for help from a disintegrating personality (and it can be viewed for profit in no other way), then someone needs to feel ashamed for ignoring and gaining from Carey's pain, and for foisting this shambling monstrosity on unsuspecting 12-year-old girls."—Film Freak Central

DEAR DIARY: I HOPE MY WIFE DOESN'T READ YOU!

Once upon a time, there was a Romanian teenager (let's call him Adrian) who heard that a single man could perform no more than 10,000 sexual acts in a lifetime. Well, Adrian wasn't going to take that one lying down. And so, as an adult, he started a diary. A diary with one purpose only: to record each and every sexual act he ever had. Adrian tended to his diary faithfully over the years; no sexual incident was too small or ill-advised to evade entry in his journal.

This eventually led to some good news for Adrian: at the age of 60, he was closing in on the magic 10,000 acts number. That was the good news.

The not so good news—just as he was closing in on his magic number, Adrian's wife found his diary and its voluminous entries concerning her hubby's sexual activity. The even worse news was that apparently less than a third of the entries actually involved her.

My Achy Breaky Heart

To be fair, she was credited as being a participant in roughly 3,000 events, more than any other participant, and, if you add up the time involved, it would almost certainly seem to be a healthy amount. But then there were those 7,000 other incidents. Maybe if there were just fewer other incidents Adrian could have explained away some of those couple thousand events that just meant nothing. But the percentages were against him.

Adrian's wife filed for divorce, citing overwhelming evidence of her husband's infidelity. For his part, Adrian told a Romanian newspaper that he regretted that he'll be losing his family over this. And also his diary, which was taken as evidence.

Source: Ananova

* * *

FANCY MEETING YOU HERE

A Romanian man and wife were talking to each other on their cell phones. He was telling her that he was at his parents' house, doing a bunch of chores. She was telling him that she was at home, in bed, because she wasn't feeling well. So it was mildly inconvenient for both when they bumped into each other, while still on the phone, at the seaside resort both had snuck off to without the other. The couple reported that they went home to try to patch things up but would probably divorce. Yeah, that's not much of a surprise.

Source: Ananova

* * *

"The easiest person to deceive is oneself."
—**Edward Bulwer-Lytton**

WHAT THE HACK?

E veryone knows that computer skills are dreadfully important to the next generation of workers. And to signal the importance of computer skills, the Economy, Trade, and Industry Ministry of Japan planned a computer competition for high school and vocational college students. The competition would pit teams of young computer geniuses against each other. The goal was to build security measures for their computers and then defend their computers against security incursions while simultaneously attempting to overcome the security measures devised by other teams.

In the real world, we call that hacking. And it's sort of, you know, *illegal*. In Japan, if you're caught hacking, you can get a year in the slammer (in a space even smaller than a Japanese hotel room) and a fine of 500,000 yen (about $4,200). Losses due to computer crime, which includes hacking into computer security systems will cost businesses in the United States an estimated $2.8 billion in 2003, and billions more worldwide.

The ministry was subsequently swamped with angry calls suggesting that it was encouraging cybercrime rather than teaching Japan's youth that hacking wasn't a very nice thing to do. The ministry eventually agreed and pulled the plug on the contest. Ironically, one of the reasons the ministry had planned the contest was to promote computer security. This is not unlike promoting fire safety by letting teenagers set off a series of uncontrolled fires.

Sources: Associated Press, USA *Today*

DUMB MUNICIPAL CODES IN ACTION

Some people can't handle alcohol very well, and not because they've had some sort of industrial accident that has left them without the opposable thumbs needed for truly competent handling of beer steins. We mean that they're alcoholics, burdened with a disease that makes them especially susceptible to the addictive nature of drink. Alas, the way most people find out they are alcoholics is by drinking themselves into trouble. It's sort of a catch-22 that way.

A Pack of Kools and Some Kool-Aid

"Catch-22" is also the way to describe the situation faced by the owner of the Keep It Simple club in Edmonton, Canada, in August of 2003. Keep It Simple was a "bar" for recovering alcoholics, in that it provided all the ambiance of a bar (bars being a second home for many alcoholics, for obvious reasons) but without all that troublesome alcohol. Part of the ambiance, along with the pretzel bowls and pool tables, is the haze of cigarette smoke: Recovering alcoholics are notorious smokers. Sure, it's trading one addiction for another, but on the other hand, smoking two packs of cigarettes won't cause you to wrap your car around a tree like a case of cheap beer will. In the short-term, it's an understandable trade.

But Edmonton has smoking laws, and the Keep it Simple bar had a problem: The only bars you can smoke in are the ones that serve alcohol. So, in order to allow smoking on the premises, the bar had to apply for a liquor license.

A.K.A. the Quibbling Commission

Fine, said Tom Charbonneau, the co-owner of Keep it Simple; he went to get the liquor license, but didn't plan to actually use it. When the Alberta Gaming and Liquor Commission heard about that, however, they refused to give over the license. "They weren't looking for a liquor license, they were looking for a smoking license," said Alberta Gaming spokeswoman Marilyn Carlyle-Helms. Not that they give out smoking licenses. That'd just be silly.

Thus the catch-22: Recovering alcoholics smoke. A non-alcoholic bar wants them to be able to smoke, in part so they won't head over to bars that serve alcohol. But in order to allow these patrons to smoke, this non-alcoholic bar has to sell booze. Which, in the case of recovering alcoholics, is defeating the whole purpose of giving them a booze-free bar environment.

Smoking Allowed

"If they say I have to serve a 12-pack, I will buy a 12-pack of beer, sell it for $5 a can, call all the media, stand in front of our sober club and pour it all out on the ground, just to show them how ridiculous it is," Charbonneau said. We say, you go, Charbonneau. Normally we're not much for folks charring their lungs, even folks who benefit from universal health care, but given the choice between recovering alcoholics charring their lungs someplace where no one's drinking, or charring their lungs where everyone's abusing their liver, well, one's the smart(er) choice. Or at the very least, one makes the roads safer after the bars close.

Source: *Edmonton Journal*

AS FAR AS YOU KNOW, THIS ARTICLE IS 100% ORIGINAL

The Internet is a powerful tool for research—anyone with a computer connection can access thousands of newspapers, magazines, and Web sites from which to suck down information on anything from quantum physics to chicken recipes to (ahem) hundreds upon hundreds of stories of people doing really dumb things all around the globe. But while the Internet makes it easy to research, it also makes it easy to plagiarize—particularly for college students who assume that their professors will never know if they cut and paste significant portions of someone else's work into their own paper, or even if they simply turn in a term paper they've found online.

Here's a hint for you, kids: they're on to you. One article about online plagiarism, entitled "Probing for Plagiarism in the Virtual Classroom" was published in the online version of *Syllabus*, a technology magazine for academics, in May 2003. It detailed a number of ways those crafty kids were wantonly plagiarizing material they found online—and how online tools also made it easier to expose those who plagiarized.

Enough Irony to Cure Anemia

So how's this for irony: turns out that this article on plagiarism was—oh, come on, you can guess—plagiarized itself. Whole chunks were lifted out of a previous article, "Maintaining Academic Integrity in Online Education," by Michael Heberling, president of Baker

College for Graduate Studies in Flint, Michigan. And how did Heberling find out about the plagiarism? Online, of course. There are so many layers of irony (and plagiarism) here that it's hard to know where to start.

Confronted with the lifted passages, one of the coauthors of the *Syllabus* article maintained the somewhat contradictory dual excuses of "it was unintentional" and "we had deadline pressure." Interestingly, those excuses sound awfully familiar. People have been lifting those from other plagiarists for *years*.

Sources: *San Antonio Express-News*, *The Chronicle of Higher Education* (See? Sources! We have nothing to hide!)

* * *

F IS FOR FAILURE

We're all used to hearing about kids who fail literacy tests, but when a superintendent of schools fails one, it's really a cause for concern. Wilfredo T. Laboy, superintendent of schools for Lawrence, Kansas, failed the state's required literacy test—for the third time. Ironically, Laboy had recently placed a couple dozen teachers on leave for failing an English proficiency test. Asked why he failed his own test, Laboy gave excuses that should sound familiar to any test-taker, including a lack of preparation and concentration. Back to the books!

Source: Associated Press

TIPS FOR STUPID CRIMINALS

*Because without these tips, they'd have to get,
you know, real jobs.*

HE'LL BE CALLING FROM A CELL,
NOT ON ONE
Today's tip: Keep your identity private.

Pedro decided he needed a car, so he took one at gunpoint from its owner. He also stole the cell phone that happened to be in the car. So far, so good (for Pedro, not the car's owner). But it seems that the owner of the car really wanted it back. So he called Pedro on the stolen cell and negotiated a ransom for the car: about $350. But where to leave the money?

No problem: Pedro gave the car's owner his bank account number. From there things went downhill pretty quickly for Pedro. "The owner rushed to us asking for help," investigator Jose Bezerra said to Reuters news agency. "It was no Swiss account, so we quickly found him."

Now Pedro has no phone, no car, and no freedom. At least he still has his bank account.

Source: Reuters

A HARD KNOCK LIFE

In Berlin in July 2003, jobs were not easy to come by—but "Fiona" needed a job. She made a trip to the government-run job agency with realistically low expectations. Just about any job would do.

Except for the one the job agency suggested for her—a job in a brothel. Yes, and not as a maid.

It was all a crazy misunderstanding said a spokesperson for the agency. "They were looking for someone to work in a massage parlor. We didn't know it was a brothel." Well, maybe a quick hit over at the brothel's Web site would have cleared things up.

One of the "enticing" lines on the site proclaims to prospective clients, "We'll spoil you with hot kisses, tender and loving massages, or no-holds-barred sex." Really, it says that. We (*ahem*) checked ourselves. No, we won't tell you the Web site. But let's just say that when a place of business with a Web site like this notes that it's in the market for "nice, pretty, unmarried women between the ages of 18 and 35," they're probably not looking for someone to do filing.

"You should see the job as an important challenge in your life," the Web site suggests. Well, that's one way of looking at it. Fiona decided she wasn't up for the challenge. "It really is a bit much if the job center assumes that the best thing is for you to try your luck in a whorehouse," she quipped to the newspaper *Tageszeitung*. One wonders what the next job on the list might have been.

Sources: Reuters, Agence France-Presse, and that Web site that we're not going to tell you about. So don't ask!

DOUBLE YOUR PLEASURE

Chew on this: in March 2003, the Wm. Wrigley Jr. Company (purveyors of the Doublemint, Juicy Fruit, and Wrigley's Spearmint chewing gum brands), patented a new type of chewable treat. In patent 6,531,114, the gum company describes "a method for treating erectile dysfunction in an individual comprising the steps of providing a chewing gum composition that includes a therapeutically effective amount of sildenafil citrate in the chewing gum composition."

Translation: Viagra gum.

The patent says that putting a stick of the stuff in your mouth causes the sildenafil citrate (the generic name for Viagra) "to be released from the chewing gum composition into the oral cavity of the individual." Each stick would contain anywhere from 20 to 100 mg of the drug. For maximum effectiveness, you'd need to chew the gum for no less than two minutes— say, the playing time of Marvin Gaye's "Let's Get It On" (or perhaps "Sexual Healing" would be the more appropriate choice)—no less than a half hour before following Marvin's advice.

The patent does not address how desperately smacking on gum for several minutes before sex could actually be conducive to the act itself.

No word as to what this new gum might be branded. Sadly, "Big Red" is already taken.

Sources: *Scientific American*, U.S. Patent and Trademark Office

HISTORICAL DUMBOSITY: DONKEY KONG KRAZINESS

W e're setting the time machine back to the magical year of 1983: a time of pastel clothing, a cross dresser named Boy George topping the musical charts, and all the Ewoks you could eat! It was also the era in which a tiny company called Nintendo of America released an arcade game, Donkey Kong, that took the country by storm.

Gorilla Tactics

In the game—if for some reason you've blocked all memory of it from your mind—the player controls Mario, a humble Italian plumber, who races up a series of ramps to rescue his girlfriend, who has been kidnapped by a gorilla, the Donkey Kong of the title. As our intrepid plumber scales the ramps, the gorilla throws barrels down at him to stop his progress. It's said that Donkey Kong's creator, Shigeru Miyamoto, based the game on the classic "Beauty and the Beast" story, although few if any versions of the story up to that point featured gorillas, Italian plumbers, or barrels hurled down ramps.

But who cares? The game was a huge smash and earned Nintendo of America $100 million in its first year. The company was busy stuffing money in its pockets just as fast as it could in the form of licensing agreements, including versions of the game for various consoles and computer platforms. The game was sucking in quarters, dollars, millions. Things just couldn't go wrong. Until entertainment giant MCA, owner of Universal Studios, decided to sue Nintendo.

Kong of All They Survey

Why? Simple: Universal Studios made the classic 1933 movie *King Kong*. MCA decided that the name "Donkey Kong" infringed on its copyright for *King Kong*. That being the case, MCA felt that Nintendo owed it a little something—say, all the profits made from the game and its various licensings. Oh, and MCA wanted Nintendo to destroy all existing unsold Donkey Kong inventory—just to make sure. Nintendo, quite obviously taken aback, and with no wish to turn over all its booty, started researching all it could find out about MCA, Universal Studios, and *King Kong*.

Media Giant Killer

And, wouldn't you know, Nintendo found out something *very* interesting: namely, that MCA *didn't* own the rights to *King Kong;* the rights had lapsed at some point in the past. And, not only did MCA and Universal know that, but in a previous, unrelated lawsuit, they pointed out that *King Kong* was in the public domain. Armed with this knowledge, Nintendo told MCA to go hang. MCA, enraged like a gorilla hurling barrels, sued anyway. But like the very creature it tried to litigate out of existence, MCA fell hard at the end. Ultimately, the courts ruled in favor of Nintendo and MCA was required to pay Nintendo $1.8 million in damages. That's a lot of bananas.

Sources: Gamespy.com, Snopes.com

TIPS FOR STUPID CRIMINALS

*Because our lawyers tell us we can't legally be held
responsible, that's why.*

SPELING MATERS
Today's tip: Good spelling matters.

If "Jerry" was known for anything, it was for being
a poor speller. This worked to his disadvantage in
June 2003, when it became clear to him that he
was on his way out of his job as a maintenance man at
a gas station in Napavine, Washington. Jerry decided
to go out with a bang, and later in the day, a bomblike
object was discovered in a closet at the gas station.
Near the would-be explosive was a note: "The bom
will bloe if you touch it."

To be fair to Jerry, "bom" *is* an actual word, defined
in Webster's Revised Unabridged Dictionary as "a
large American serpent, so called from the sound it
makes." But in this particular context, it was pretty
clear that no large American serpent was present. And
"bloe" just isn't a word, no matter how you slice it. All
signs pointed to a bad speller, possibly a disgruntled
one. So that was how Jerry got himself arrested and
charged with malicious placement of an imitation
explosive device.

If he's convicted, he'll go to jale.

Source: Associated Press

THE REALLY STUPID QUIZ: THOSE DISTURBING ANIMALS!

Look! It's another Really Stupid Quiz! One of these really happened; the other two are just shaggy dog tales. You pick out the purebred from the mutts.

1. A man claiming to be a herpetologist from the St. Louis Zoo was arrested at Newark International Airport when a snake he was transporting vomited up several plastic bags filled with heroin. The snake, a Brazilian rainbow boa, had been fed a small rabbit that had been stuffed with the bags of drugs. The drugs were discovered as baggage handlers took the snake out of the cargo hold of the airplane and noticed the plastic bags in the snake's carry cage, along with the remains of the rabbit. The snake's owner was held on drug charges as well as a charge of animal cruelty. The St. Louis Zoo later told the police the accused smuggler was not on its staff.

2. Call it the bat's revenge: two Mexican teenagers inadvertently cut off the power supply to their Baja California town after one of the bats they were shooting at winged toward a nearby transformer station before expiring. Its carcass fell into one of the transformers and burst into flame, triggering an automatic safety shutdown of the station. The station crew had to remove the charred remains. Power stayed down for several hours; the boys were charged with malicious mischief but the charges were later dropped on the condition they surrender their weapons to the local police.

3. A man in Germany awoke to suspicious sounds in his garden. Fearing a burglary, he phoned the police, who came around and searched for evidence of a break-in. What they found was two hedgehogs making love. Strange as this may sound, it's not the first time mating hedgehogs have been mistaken for burglars: in New Zealand in 2002, eight policemen, accompanied by dogs, searched for a burglar only to discover the small, amorous animals.

Which one is really stupid?

Answer page 311.

Source: Ananova

* * *

"If there are no stupid questions, then what kind of questions do stupid people ask? Do they get smart just in time to ask questions?"

—Scott Adams

"The stupider the peasant, the better the horse understands him."

—Anton Pavlovich Chekhov

THANK GOD IT WASN'T A MEDICAL EXAM

Come with us now to India. In a town called Kavali in the Andhra Pradesh state, a young man we'll call "Sameer" is in a theater watching a film, *Gangotri,* in which the hero of the film dresses up as a woman in order to take a school exam for the film's heroine. This strikes Sameer as a clever idea, but he doesn't seem to recognize that movies are unrealistic representations of life in which people do things like walking on walls or bursting into song.

Hey, Sis, Can I Borrow That Pink Number?

This certain lack of comprehension goes a long way to explain why our friend Sameer was arrested not long after watching *Gangtori* for attempting to take his sister's school entrance exams. He put on a wig and women's clothing and actually managed to get into the entrance hall and take the test. However, one of the examiners noticed that Sameer's signature on the test didn't match the signature they had on file. Also he didn't look much like his sister. This *might* have been because Sameer was 22 years old and his sister was 12 years old.

Sameer was arrested for impersonation and forgery. But look at the bright side: if Sameer was getting his big ideas from movies and actually thought an adult man could pass as a preadolescent girl, just how *useful* do you think his test answers would have been to his sister?

Sources: *Deccan Chronicle,* Ananova

HOW NOT TO HAIL A TAXI

You remember that scene in *Midnight Cowboy* where a taxi nearly hits Dustin Hoffman and he starts pounding on the hood of the taxi, shouting, "I'm walking here!" Or if you don't remember it because the movie came out 33 years ago, then you know it from the various parodies of it in everything from *Forrest Gump* to Disney's *Hercules*. Point is, you know it. It's become the accepted way of harassing overaggressive taxi drivers the world over.

Well, "Jae," a Korean businessman, apparently left his "how to harass a taxi driver" instructions at home, because when a taxi nearly ran him down in Manila, he decided to forgo the usual pounding and shouting and instead decided on an alternate method of protest: he flashed his genitals at the taxi driver.

Why the Southern Exposure?

We feel this choice of expression is enigmatic. We would think that of all the body parts to present in this situation, the ones you'd least want to expose would be the most sensitive ones of all.

Exhibiting one's genitals in public is usually confined to strip clubs, rock festivals, and Mardi Gras. A passing policeman caught Jae in his moment of undress and hauled him in to the police station. Jae apparently cursed and shouted the whole way. But we're willing to bet he kept the privates private once he got there. Jail's the last place you want to be flashing anybody.

Source: Reuters

HOW TO ANNOY
A JUDGE, TIP #4,655

We can understand why people on probation would like to get off probation a little early. Probation is such a drag: there's always someone checking up on you, asking you what you've been doing, who you're hanging out with—it's like they think you're a criminal or something.

But if you want to get off of probation early, you need to have a really excellent excuse. And a really excellent excuse is not what "Lionel" had when he faced a Broward County, Florida, circuit judge and asked to be let off his yearlong probation when he still had four months to go.

> **Judge:** "Why should I let you off early?" (or words to that effect)
> **Lionel:** "Because I don't eat poppy seed bagels."
> **Judge:** "What?" (or a word to that effect)
> **Lionel:** "Well, I really love poppy seed bagels. But I'm worried that if I eat them, they'll cause me to test positive for drug use. So I eat plain bagels instead. Surely this voluntary deprivation is proof of my saintliness and an excellent reason to be let off probation."
> **Judge:** "You're insane. Get the hell out of my courtroom." (or words to that effect)

Bet you don't get any credit for near beer, either.

Source: *South Florida Sun-Sentinel*

TIPS FOR STUPID CRIMINALS

Because there's always room for improvement.

DUBYA DOLLARS
Today's tip: When attempting to bribe your way to freedom, don't use counterfeit bills.

Our thief, "Frankie," picked the wrong house to knock over. Frank allegedly snuck into the Des Moines, Iowa, home of 87-year-old Rozetta Lee in the early morning hours by cutting the screen on her bedroom window. Lee awoke and started screaming. Her son Charles, 53, who was sleeping in the basement heard her.

According to Charles, upon finding Frankie in his mom's room, he grabbed him and started hauling him outside "to whoop him a little." Frankie, a decade and a half younger but apparently not confident in his ability to defend himself, tried to make Charles a deal: he'd give him $100 to forget it all happened. And maybe the plan would have worked, too, if it weren't for the fact that the face on the $100 bill wasn't Ben "It's All About the Benjamins" Franklin, but rather George "Dubya" Bush. And whatever one's opinion of the 43rd President of the United States, we can all agree that on a $100 bill, the man is literally worthless.

So no freedom for Frankie; Des Moines police came and picked him up and charged him with second-degree burglary. His bail was $13,000. Wonder if he tried to pay that with Dubya bills, too.

Source: Associated Press

HAPPY BIRTHDAY, DUMB-ASS

Olaf" was turning 40, a year in which one traditionally celebrates the onset of a midlife crisis, that all-purpose excuse that allows you to do a bunch of inadvisable things like bungee jumping, purchasing impractical cars, or dating your children's friends, with the excuse that you're freaking out because you've finally realized your hair isn't coming back. To commemorate the occasion, Olaf's friends had planned a surprise birthday party for him.

It Comes As No Surprise

Olaf found out about the surprise birthday party, and perhaps in attempt to capitalize on his newfound ability to act in a juvenile fashion, decided to pull a surprise act of his own. Unbeknownst to his friends, Olaf sneaked up and waited outside the cabin where the party was to take place, and when enough people had shown up, he took his shotgun and shot it into the air, scaring the hell out of his pals.

What a prankster! After he scared his friends, Olaf popped out of the shadows to take credit for his mischief, and as he did so, he tripped, and the shotgun went off again. Six of his pals went off to the hospital. So did Olaf, who was not injured but was described as being in shock because he'd just shot six of his friends. The party was canceled. Olaf can expect to spend his 41st birthday alone. That's a midlife crisis for you.

Source: Reuters

HE'LL NEED ONE HECK OF A WIRELESS CONNECTION

The Italian government wanted something from Nicola Valeriani: it wanted him to buy a new computer. The Italians, and not unreasonably so, believe that computer literacy is the wave of the future. For today's young Italians to succeed in the world markets, they would need the skills that would have them known as pioneers on the cutting edge of technology.

To this end, the Italians gave grants to select 16-year-olds to purchase high-tech equipment; in June 2003, Valeriani was one of those selected. "As part of an initiative by my ministry known as the 'Fly with Interne' project you have been selected to receive a grant to help you get online and buy a new PC," read a letter to Valeriani from Innovations Minister (there's a gig for you) Lucio Stanca. It was an offer the government figured Valeriani couldn't refuse.

He refused. Sort of. Turns out Nicola Valeriani wasn't 16. He was 116. Or *would* have been, had he not been dead for nearly 30 years at the time. Valeriani, who had been born in 1887 and who had fought in both World Wars, had gone offline permanently in 1974, back when the Internet was basically an inside joke between a couple of house-sized mainframes at the U.S. Department of Defense. Valeriani's daughter, no spring chicken herself, returned the check.

The cause for the error? According to the Italian Innovations Ministry, it was a computer glitch.

Source: Ananova

THE RUSSIAN VERSION OF SING-SING

Hey, you don't know how it happened, but *somehow*, you've managed to land yourself a spell in a Russian prison, with nothing to look forward to but beets three times a day and a dog-eared copy of *The Gulag Archipelago*. Sure you're innocent. *Everybody's* innocent in prison, pal. The question is: how are you going to get out?

Easy: sing. In May 2003, the Moscow radio station Troika looked at the popularity of the various "Pop Idol" shows around the world and decided that they were all doing it wrong. After all, it's not like these fresh-scrubbed young Westerners singing painfully earnest ballads really *lose* anything if they don't win—they just go back to singing at the local dinner theater. The contest needed a little drama. It needed a little excitement. It needed singers with desire, with drive, with convictions.

You Know, Aleksandr Solzhenitsyn Had a Fabulous Singing Voice

So they hatched a plan: all across the 748-prison Russian penal system were more than one million inhabitants with lots of time to work on some songs. So, Russian prisoners would compete in a singing contest in which the winner would get fabulous prizes, including his or her freedom and a recording contract. The losers, presumably, would be returned to their dank and festering holes. Prison officials had been asked to disqualify the *really* bad eggs, but the definition of "really bad" seems to be on something of a sliding scale, since several convicted killers were allowed to croon for their chance at a musical acquittal.

Tastelessly exploitative? Not according to a Troika spokesperson, who reasoned, "There's lots of talented people out there in those prisons, and this is just the way for them to be discovered." But don't they realize that fame is a prison, too? Just with better bathing facilities.

In any event, remember: if you're ever thrown into a Russian slammer, start working on those scales. Ask your cellmate to help. Maybe you two could sing a duet.

Source: Ananova

* * *

ALIAS, ME

How carefully do the police check names on their police warrants? In Pinellas County, Florida, not carefully enough. A man was held for six days on a 33-year-old narcotics possession warrant because his first and last name matched that of the wanted man. The middle name was different, but police said they thought the middle name might have been switched as an alias. That's a pretty subtle alias. The man was finally released when his fingerprints proved him innocent. We smell a lawsuit!

Source: Associated Press

SO MUCH FOR PUPPY LOVE

A dog is man's best friend, but the converse is not always true. Look at what people do: they leave their dogs at home all day, alone, while they go off to work or school and have full, engaging lives. When the humans *do* come home, they're so tired from all that working they hardly have time to spend with their puppy pals. And if the dog does manage to guilt its master into a walk, it's usually a quick trip to the nearest fire hydrant. A dog's life really is a dog's life; it's not just a convenient expression.

So thought German artist Karl-Friedrich Lentze. "Some dogs only get a five minute walkies on the lead and that's not enough even to sniff another canine, let alone indulge in a bit of fun," he said in a business application to the City of Berlin.

His proposed business? A dog brothel.

Dogs Just Want to Have Fun

Lentze's plan: for about $40, those poor neglected stay-at-home dogs would get, well, you know, *sex*.

The city council was not amused, but the rejection was, shall we say, based on extremely spurious, not to mention highly judgmental, reasons. "Dog sex is for the purpose of reproduction only," a report by a city official maintained. "There is no evidence of a problem with sexual frustration among the city's dogs."

This contention might come as a surprise to anyone whose leg has received the amorous attention of a Jack Russell terrier. But Berlin's city fathers planned for that objection. "When dogs rub themselves on people's legs it is just a result of boredom and an attempt to show who's boss," the report maintained.

So all those *Berlinerhunden* are just plain out of luck. "A visit to the brothel would only reinforce a dog's sense of importance and make him more trouble-some, not less," the city council report stated in its rejection of Lentze's business. But perhaps it's for the best. Imagine being a Berliner caught outside a brothel and trying to explain to people that you're just there to pick up a dog. People would run screaming.

Source: Ananova

* * *

NOW HEAR THIS

A Brazilian man had a severe ear infection, so he went to the local clinic to get it looked at. After some time, he thought he heard his name called, so he went into the doctor. Turns out the doctor had called someone else—who had come in for a vasectomy—which our man allowed the doctor to perform! When asked why he let a doctor fiddle with equipment that had so little to do with his ear, the man replied that he'd just assumed the infection had spread.

That's some ear infection!

Source: Reuters

DUMB MOVIE FESTIVAL:
FREDDY GOT FINGERED (2001)

Our Entry: *Freddy Got Fingered*, starring Tom Green and Rip Torn

The Plot (Such As It Is): A diminishingly youthful cartoonist (Green) antagonizes everyone and everything around him, especially his father (Torn), whom he accuses of molesting his brother (the Freddy of the title). Along the way Green does some astoundingly avile things involving barnyard animals and umbilical cords that are not only not worth describing, but probably shouldn't even be thought about. Green also cowrote and directed this film, which is generally regarded as the worst movie of the 21st century to date.

Fun Fact: When Tom Green made this movie, he was married to Drew Barrymore, who has a small cameo in the film. Now he's not. Coincidence?

Total North American Box Office: $14,249,005 (source: The-Numbers.com). Frighteningly enough, the film cost $15 million, which means after home video release, it probably actually became profitable. That noise you hear is one of the seals of the Apocalypse being cracked.

The Critics Rave!

"Green is perhaps the only person on earth who could make a moviegoer actually nostalgic for the subtle intellectual brilliance of Pauly Shore."—*Sacramento News & Review*

"How bad are we talking about? Consider this: At a recent preview screening for an audience top-heavy with members of the target youth-market demographic, the picture generated a steady stream of walkouts. And when the film finally, mercifully ended, the hardy few who remained were in such a hurry to leave that—are you ready for this? are you sitting down?—many left behind their souvenir, movie tie-in T-shirts."—*San Francisco Examiner*

"If you go to see this movie, Green will earn the money to make another one. That's between you and your conscience."—Jam! Showbiz

"Putting [Green] in the director's chair is like handing a drunk gorilla the keys to the monkey house—the result is complete chaos, a deafening free-for-all of screaming, hollering, and fluid-spraying."—Reel.com

"This movie doesn't scrape the bottom of the barrel. This movie isn't the bottom of the barrel. This movie isn't below the bottom of the barrel. This movie doesn't deserve to be mentioned in the same sentence with barrels."
—*Chicago Sun-Times*

TIPS FOR STUPID CRIMINALS

It's time again for Tips for Stupid Criminals! Because smart criminals don't need tips, do they?

THROW THE BOOK AT ME, WHY DON'T YOU?

Today's tip: When being sentenced for a crime, don't taunt your judge into giving you the maximum sentence.

You wouldn't think someone would need this tip. But it would have come in handy for "Joe," who faced Judge Craig Doran in New York for sentencing on a burglary charge (he'd stolen jewelry from his girlfriend and her parents). Judge Doran accused Joe of being unremorseful, and Joe, all riled up, dared the judge to do his worst. "Are you gonna sentence me to the max?" Joe said, full of the bravado that makes for a great story in the big house recreation yard. "Is that what you're getting at? Go ahead! You're going to give it to me anyway!" Doran, apparently an obliging judge if there ever was one, sentenced Joe to the slammer for the maximum seven years.

Joe's lawyers maintained that their client was indeed remorseful. They probably should have checked with Joe for confirmation on that.

Source: Ananova

YOU FOUND
WHAT IN MY FREEZER?

What's in your freezer right now? No, don't go *look*. Do it from memory. Not so easy to remember, is it? And you're probably forgetting that bag of mixed vegetables that's been in there longer than you've been married, or the box of diet Fudgsicles that came to live in the chilly confines of your freezer roughly the same time Eric the Red landed in Greenland. Let's face it, it's easy to lose track of what's in there.

But some items are more memorable than others. So we wonder what was with up with "Sal" and "Eva," two citizens of De Leon Springs, Florida. One day, officers from the Florida Fish and Wildlife Conservation Commission came to their door and asked to look through their freezer. Just a few hours before, Sal and Eva had been written up for shooting at deer from their car; they'd been found in their car with a shotgun and open beer cans shortly after officers heard gunshots in the Ocala National Forest. Now the officers wanted to make sure the two of them weren't in possession of illegal venison.

What Did They Have to Lose?

Sal and Eva gave them permission to look because, as it happens, there was no venison in the freezer. But Sal and Eva forgot about something *else* they had in the freezer: two plastic bags filled with a total of about a pound of marijuana. That's a lot of pot. Even if you're baked to the gills, we're betting you'd probably remember where you'd stashed *that.*

What an interesting collection of charges Sal and Eva ended up with: felony possession of marijuana *and* taking a deer at night, plus discharging a firearm on a highway and possession of an open container.

Kind of makes you want to go check out your freezer doesn't it? You know, just to be *sure.*

Source: *Ft. Myers News-Press*

* * *

SMOKE 'EM IF YOU'VE GOT 'EM

The two Austrian customs officers' jobs included confiscating black market cigarettes and then destroying them. However, they weren't supposed to destroy them by smoking them. Or give them to friends and family. Or hold smoking parties in the customs office with confiscated liquor to lubricate the partiers. Just a hunch, but this is probably why these two customs officers were charged with misuse of office.

Source: Ananova

YOU OUGHTA BE IN PICTURES. OR NOT.

One of the great mantras of the Internet is "information wants to be free." Now, most people think that means that all those MP3s and pictures of scantily clad people doing scantily clad things want to be downloaded onto your hard drive without you having to pay for it. Well, that is one interpretation—one that anyone with a copyright gets a little twitchy about. But we're thinking more about the personal and *dark* side of that particular maxim, which is that anything you ever do on the Internet is going to come back and kick you right in the gut when you least expect it.

Just Her Type—Dumb As a Post
Ask British politician Phil Grayson about this one. In March 2003, Grayson started receiving e-mail from "Julie Masters," who claimed to be a 23-year-old woman who liked older men, a category for which the 45-year-old Grayson was eminently qualified. Apparently unaware that the number of actual hot 23-year-old women soliciting older men for attention on the entire Internet could be counted on one hand, and that in any event the very last thing a married, father-of-two politician wants to do is get involved with a presumed younger woman he's never even seen, Grayson began an e-mail correspondence that included steamy fantasies, which we can all agree are better left unsaid.

But what fun are stories without pictures? Apparently

no fun at all, because in addition to the fantasies, Grayson included pictures in his e-mails, and not the sort you show people when they come over for dinner, unless your idea of predinner entertainment is to show your guests pictures of yourself wearing suspenders, tights, and no underwear. (In which case, *never* invite us for dinner.)

Seduced and Betrayed

This is where that "information wants to be free" thing kicks in. Turns out "Julie Masters" was not the special friend she claimed to be, because she sent the pictures to each and every member of the borough council of which Grayson was a member. This was of course very bad news for Grayson; imagine coming into work and realizing that everyone in your office has seen you naked. It's not so much of a problem if you're a stripper, but how many of us are? And as bad as it was for Grayson, think about it from the other end of things; your coworker wants to talk to you about issues for the next meeting and all she is doing is picturing you in tights and suspenders. And no underwear. It's distracting, to say the least.

Faced with scandal, Grayson resigned from his political party in August 2003 and admitted to the press, "I was stupid and naive to do what I did." Well, yes. Give a thought the next time you're sending something across the Net that maybe you don't want the rest of us to see—and that the rest of us, to be fair, would probably be better off not seeing anyway. Information wants to be free, whether we all want it to be or not.

Sources: *London Evening Standard, Register* (U.K.)

HISTORICAL DUMBOSITY: WHEN WILL THEY EVER LEARN?

I magine, for a moment, you are the emperor of Europe. Nice continent, Europe; lots of fine cheeses, exceptional autobahns, and the occasional bit of sculpture. But over there, on the periphery, lies Russia, taunting you with its existence. And you start thinking to yourself, isn't Russia part of Europe, too? Well then, I should be emperor of that, too!

Just hold your horses, your majesty (and hold your infantry, and cannon, and tanks, and artillery) because here's a fact: Russia is the black hole of European wars. It's the roach motel of European empires: they check in but they don't check out. Russia is where dreams of European conquest come to die, usually with frostbite and dysentery. And if you don't believe it, just ask Napoleon and Hitler, both of whom foolishly decided to show Russia what for, and both of whom—through lack of planning, underappreciation of Russian tenacity, and general stupidity—saw their empires get cashed in for their pains.

Napoleon First

As you may know, in 1811, Napoleon was on top of the world, the European part of it, anyway: his empire ranged from the Italian peninsula to the Baltic Sea. He was trying to force Great Britain to its knees with a blockade. That was no good for the Russians, who depended on British trade, so finally Czar Alexander said "enough" to the blockade. Well, Napoleon couldn't have that. People start disobeying you, and the next thing you know, you're stuck on Elba playing chess with your guards. And that's just no good.

So Napoleon decided to "persuade" Alexander to his point of view in 1812 by parking a "Grand Army" of 600,000 on Russia's doorstep (by which we mean, of course, Poland). The idea here was that, confronted with the greatest army the world had ever seen, Russia would see reason. And if it didn't, well, that was okay with Napoleon, too: "I know Alexander," Napoleon said. "I once had influence over him; it will come back. If not, let destiny be accomplished and let Russia be crushed under my hatred of England."

Well, Russia didn't seem to understand his logic, so in June 1812, against the advice of his advisers, Napoleon's Grand Army stomped onto Russian soil. Napoleon was so confident of victory that he expected his adventure to be over in twenty days, so that he didn't bother to lay in substantial supplies for his army—he expected his soldiers to live off the land.

Hey, Who Ate the Last Potato?

Problems cropped up immediately. First off, it was summer in Russia, and it was hot—*really* hot. Second, Russia had terrible roads, which meant the entire army had to stick to the roads that were usable. This was no good for foraging off the land, since the troops in front ate everything available, leaving nothing for the troops behind. Not that there was much of anything to begin with: the Russian troops, rather than facing the Grand Army and conveniently dying like Napoleon had been planning, kept retreating—and laying waste to the Russian countryside as they ran.

Within a month, the Grand Army, still chasing after the Russians, was not so grand. Soldiers were weak from hunger and falling ill from various diseases, most prominently typhus and dysentery. And it wasn't just the soldiers: more than 10,000 of the army's horses had died of starvation.

Napoleon finally caught the Russians on the out-skirts of Moscow, three months after his army crossed the border. By this time, more than 200,000 of his sol-diers were either dead or out of commission. Still, he had enough men to finally have a battle: the Battle of Borodino, a remarkably vicious battle where the Napoleon's army killed off 44,000 Russians in a single day (and lost 30,000 of their own). Napoleon won the battle and thus earned the right to enter the city of Moscow, which for him was good. But when he entered it, it was on fire, because the Russians had torched it rather than let it fall into Napoleon's hands. Which, for him, was *bad.*

Twiddling the Imperial Thumbs
For five weeks, Napoleon hung out in the charred remains of Moscow, waiting for the czar to begin negoti-ations, which never happened. Finally, in late October, Napoleon ordered his troops back home, choosing to return the same way they had come rather than travel an alternate route—one that possibly hadn't been scorched to dust by the Russians. That was pretty dumb.

Not that it mattered much, since the retreat order came too late in the Russian climate calendar. Within three weeks, the Russian winter hit. Temperatures fell below zero. Soldiers froze as they marched. Horses died by the hundreds. And all the while, Cossacks harassed the Grand Army's flanks, picking off the weak and the sick. "Our lips stuck together," wrote one of Napoleon's soldiers. "Our nostrils froze. We seemed to be marching in a world of ice."

And how was Napoleon handling it all? He was so fearful of capture that he rode with a vial of poison around his neck. Just in case.

That's Right, Kick Him When He's Down

By the time Napoleon passed out of Russian territory, his fearsome Grand Army of 600,000 had been reduced to a sick and staggering collection of less than 100,000 men, half-crazed by cold and starvation. It was the beginning of the end for Napoleon: all the far-flung regions of his empire, emboldened by the emperor's weakened state, started rebelling. By March 1814, it was all over and Napoleon was headed to Elba, then to a brief return engagement at Waterloo, and finally to exile at that middle-of-nowhere rock known as St. Helena.

For Part II of Russian invasions, see page 308.

* * *

"For fools rush in where angels fear to tread."

—Alexander Pope

BORN TO BE BAD

Some people are born bad. And the Norwegian Traffic Insurance Federation believed Erik Solhaug Kristiansen was one of those people. On July 9, 1999, or so they contend, Erik caused a traffic accident. After injuring a bicyclist and wrecking her bike, Erik fled from the scene.

The bicyclist took more than a year to file a report about the accident, and it wasn't until 2003 that Erik was accused of the crime. But that didn't matter. Justice would be done, and Erik, the proverbial bad seed, would have it done to him.

Naturally, Erik's family rallied to his side. "The complainant has waited a whole year before pressing charges," his father protested. "How can the witnesses be so sure of what they saw, so long after the event?"

It's Inconceivable!

Oh, and there was one more small detail: "The other big question in the case is naturally that my son, the accused, cannot have been present at the scene of the accident. He was born on April 5, 2000," Mr. Kristiansen said.

A salient point. In order for Erik to have perpetrated this heinous crime, at the instant he was born he would have had to find a way to travel back in time nine months, run down the bicyclist, and make it back to his incubator, totally unsuspected.

The Traffic Insurance Federation agreed and cleared Erik of any wrongdoing. For *now*.

Sources: *Aftenposten*, Ananova

TIPS FOR STUPID CRIMINALS

Not that we expect them to listen.

THE GETAWAY
Today's tip: When robbing that bank,
keep the engine running in the getaway car.

After robbing a Cleveland bank in June 2003, our subject ran to his getaway car, only to find his driver had shut off the engine and it wouldn't start up again. Our robber leaped out of the car to steal another car, but couldn't manage that, so he ran to a nearby house and tried to steal some car keys. That didn't work either, so the man ran to Interstate 90 and tried to get cars to stop for him, but, strangely enough, no one on the interstate seemed to want to slow down for the purpose of getting carjacked by a man with a big bag of cash, who was being chased by the police. He was arrested shortly thereafter.

A law enforcement official, in a classic of understatement, had this to say: "It's very weird, and it's very stupid, but I don't think we're dealing with geniuses here."

Source: *Cleveland Plain Dealer*

THE REALLY STUPID QUIZ: BUREAUCRACY IN ACTION

Gird your loins, it's time for another Really Stupid Quiz! One of these tales of government stupidity actually happened. The other two probably could have happened, but didn't, so far as we know. It's up to you to decide which seems the most likely.

1. A Coral Gables, Florida, man accused the Florida Department of Highway Safety & Motor Vehicles of incompetence after it granted him a handicapped parking permit for being bald. "I've been noticing that people who seemed healthy have had the permits," he said, so he decided to see how difficult it was to get one by filling out the required HSMV 83039 form and forging a doctor's certification, testifying that his baldness was a debilitating illness. His permit came in the mail three weeks later. The man said he did it specifically to highlight the laxity in the system and does not intend to use the permit. A spokesperson for the HSMV says the man could be charged with falsely filing government documents but declined to state whether the department would press charges.

2. The city council of Leeds, England, decided that the local cemeteries were beginning to look a bit shabby, so it sent out letters to caretakers of the graves, telling them to clean up various flowers, vases, and other objects around the graves. One of the letters was sent to Moira Thoms. The problem: Mrs. Thoms

wasn't the grave's caretaker; she was, in fact, in the grave. Mrs. Thoms's widower angrily noted that she had been dead for three years. Embarrassed council officials apologized to Mr. Thoms.

3. A Toronto, Canada, couple were told by the Canada Customs and Revenue Agency that they could not claim child care expenses on their taxes because they had no children—even though the couple came to the meeting with the CCRA with their two children in tow. "It was absolutely incredible," said Erica Zorn, who with her husband Peter Hirsch was denied the deduction. "I was sitting there giving my son a bottle right in front of the revenue agent, who was telling me that he didn't really exist." A spokesperson for the CCRA noted that revenue field agents are required to abide by regulations even in the face of contradictory evidence and that Zorn and Hirsch would need to appeal the ruling.

Which one is really stupid?

Answer page 311.

Source: Ananova

* * *

"A stupid man's report of what a clever man says is never accurate because he unconsciously translates what he hears into something he can understand."
—**Bertrand Russsell**

DUMB MOVIE FESTIVAL: *3000 MILES TO GRACELAND* (2001)

Our Entry: *3000 Miles to Graceland*, starring Kurt Russell and Kevin Costner.

The Plot (Such As It Is): A bunch of dim-bulb thieves decide to pull a heist in Las Vegas dressed up as Elvis imitators (there's an Elvis thing going on that weekend). Then we have the usual double crosses and random violence we've been led to expect every time stupid thieves pull heists together. Subplot: Courteney Cox shows up as a single mom/floozy who steals Kurt Russell's heart and wallet, not necessarily in that order. Meant to be a career revitalizer for Costner. Failed.

Fun Fact: Since *3000 Miles* came out, Elvis Presley has had more hits on the music charts than stars Costner, Russell, Cox, Christian Slater, and David Arquette put together have had on the movie charts. You can look it up!

Total North American Box Office: $15,738,632 (source: The-Numbers.com). That's roughly a quarter of the production cost.

The Critics Rave!

"3000 Miles to Graceland shouldn't be reviewed in an arts section but rather in that portion of the newspaper dedicated to atrocities, environmental disasters and hate crimes."—Portland Oregonian

"This is so relentlessly wrongheaded and downright ugly a movie that you want to call The Hague and demand an international tribunal be formed to investigate possible crimes against humanity."—FlickFilosopher.com

"This is a terrible, horrible film, a big-budget student film with stupidity and insipidity written all over it. AOL Keyword: Suck."—hsbr.net

"One of the bloodiest and mind-bogglingly dumb action-adventures since the heyday of Steven Seagal."—Reel.com

"3000 Miles to Graceland is a slick exercise in cinema excess in which the audience is asked to pick their favourites from a gallery of low lives and hope they can elude the justice and punishment they actually deserve."—Calgary Sun

"To say that it is terribly written, amateurishly directed, sloppily edited and badly photographed is to merely scratch the surface of a fiasco so egregious it defies description." —Boxoffice.com

"Yep, 3,000 miles sure is a long way, and that's about as far off as this turgid caper is from success . . . clichéd everythings and convoluted double crosses make this one more bloated than fat Elvis."—E! Online

FROM DOO-DOO
TO DEEP DOO-DOO

How do you go from a minor ordinance violation to a felony in three quick steps? Just ask "Jan" from Bloomington, Illinois.

First, take your dog out for a walk, as Jan did. While you're out, make sure that your dog drops a load in public, which you don't bother to pick up. Also make sure your dog deposits all this doo-doo in sight of a police officer, who will naturally cite you for failure to scoop the poop. This is your ordinance violation.

Now, while the officer is writing you up for your failure to scoop, you must then walk away from the police officer and refuse to return when called back, as Jan did. Walking away from a police officer who is in the process of writing you up for an ordinance violation is technically called "obstructing police." While you are not actually obstructing a police officer, you're obstructing his *job*, which is to give you a ticket. And that's a misdemeanor.

More Arresting Behavior
Here comes the best part. After being charged for the misdemeanor, you're taken down to the police station—because you've broken the law, you see. While you're at the police station, you get it into your head, as Jan did, that this is an excellent place to kick and shove the officer who arrested you. Aside from being an interesting choice of action,

this is also aggravated battery, and that's a felony.

And for that, as Jan learned, you actually get treated to time in the county jail. And so does your dog; the county animal control took her pet after Jan got sent to the doghouse.

That's how you do it. Who knew it was that easy?

Source: *Bloomington* (IL) *Pantagraph*

* * *

ATTACK OF THE GIANT BEAVERS!

It was (one imagines) a slow day at the police station in Wiener Neustadt, Lower Austria, when the citizenry started calling en masse: there was a giant beaver rampaging through the town car park! After assembling the local fire crews and vets, the police moved in to discover the animal in question wasn't a giant beaver at all, but a kangaroo, which the police suspected was a runaway pet. The animal was quickly subdued. Meanwhile, the giant beavers on the outskirts of town, having lulled the townsfolk into a false sense of security with their decoy, plan to attack at dawn.

Source: Ananova

WHEN LIFE HANDS YOU LEMONS, MAKE SURE YOUR PERMITS ARE IN ORDER

Naples, Florida, on a sunny June day. The sun is up, the birds are singing, and the neighborhood kids, showing the sort of all-American capitalistic initiative that would make Adam Smith and J. Paul Getty sing a duet in their praises, are setting up that most hallowed of childhood summer retail establishments: the lemonade stand. And look, here come their first customers!

Naples City Police Officer #1: What's going on here, kids?

Lemonade-Selling Tyke: Golly, Mr. Policeman! We're selling lemonade! I squeezed the lemons myself!

Naples City Police Officer #2: Well, isn't that great. Tell me, have you got a permit for this stand?

Tyke: A what?

Police Officer #1: Don't play coy, buster! A permit! A license that allows you to conduct business within the city boundaries! We got a tip that says you don't got one!

Tyke (trembling): I don't got no bermit, Mr. Policeman. I just wanna sell some lemonade!

Police Officer #2: Isn't that cute. He said "bermit" instead of "permit." Well, cute's not going

to get you off the hook, sonny! It's the big house
for you! Come on, Bob, let's take him in!
Tyke: Waaaaah!

Sure, you may chuckle at this overwrought, badly
scripted scene, but think about this: in Naples, Florida,
in June 2003, police actually *did* shut down a six-year-
old girl's lemonade stand because she didn't have the
temporary business license required for anyone doing
business (temporarily) in the city. The cost of a temporary permit? $35. For each day.

Were the police cruising the mean streets of Naples
looking for children to bust? No. Get this: one of the
kid's neighbors, possibly worried that the presence of a
small retail establishment would bring down property
values, actually called the police and complained about
her enterprising little neighbor's lemonade stand.
"Normally we don't get involved in it, but once we do
get a formal request we must take action," said Naples
spokesman Al Hofgrefe. The cops who shut the kid
down felt so bad about it that one of them bought a
glass of lemonade.

Note to the neighbor: jeez, lady. Calling the cops
on a lemonade stand. That's just *mean*.

The good news here is that the city of Naples realized how stupid it was to have their cops strong-arming
first-graders and granted the little girl a business permit
at no cost. One hopes our darling little entrepreneur
sent her neighbor a refreshing complimentary glass of
lemonade with a little note that said, "Dear neighbor:
Choke on it."

Source: NBC2 News

A TAXING SITUATION

E veryone knew that Francesco Dominico La Rosa of Perth, Australia, was a drug dealer. They knew it because he was spending time in an Australian prison for dealing heroin. But just because a guy is rotting in the hole for selling smack—that most skanky of street drugs—doesn't mean he should also get dinged on his taxes. That's just not the Australian way.

Which is why La Rosa had been fighting the Australian Tax Office from his prison cell. Seems that the Tax Office claimed that in the 1994–95 tax year, La Rosa made nearly $450,000, which is a lot of money, even in Australian dollars. That being the case, the Tax Office wanted taxes assessed on that amount.

La Rosa had a different point of view. He disputed the $450,000 figure, noting that the amount included $225,000 that he believed he shouldn't have to pay taxes on. Why? Because that's the amount of money that was stolen from him in a drug deal that went south in 1995. Basically, La Rosa argued, that's $225,000 he didn't make. So he appealed the tax amount.

Wonder if He Had the Paperwork to Prove His Claim

And, what do you know, an administrative appeals tribunal agreed with La Rosa that he had been overtaxed for that year. From the point of view of the Australian courts, taking a bath on an illegal drug deal is a legitimate excuse for reducing your taxable income. A handy tip!

The irony here is that is that if De Rosa were a free man, there's probably no way he'd have gotten that $225,000 knocked off his tax bill. Because he deals drugs, you see. Admitting to that while you're a free man, even to get a slice off your tax bill, is a fine way to get hauled into the slammer. But if you're already in the slammer, what do you have to lose? So three cheers for the Australian war on drugs, and all its amusing unintended consequences.

And as for De Rosa, enjoy your tax refund, mate! We're sure the prison commissary is just waiting for your shopping spree.

Source: news.com.au

* * *

OMINOUS NEWS FOR THE IRS

The Internal Revenue Service said that Vernice Kuglin of Tennessee owed them $920,000 in back taxes, but Kuglin said that she could find nothing in the tax code that said she was liable for taxes. So she wouldn't pay. Fine, said the IRS, and took her to court, where a jury found for Kuglin, because, as one juror said, "we all felt that the prosecution didn't prove its case."

Source: *Memphis Commercial Appeal*

WELCOME TO FREEDOM, YOU'RE UNDER ARREST

I t's no big secret that many of the criminals who end up in the slammer go back to lives of crime after they're released. But usually they take a little time to do something else first. You know, like take a nap, or get a bite to eat, or have their first completely worry-free shower in years.

But not "Edwin." In what has got to be a land-speed record for recidivism, Ed was arrested at the Airway Heights Corrections Center in Washington at exactly the same time he was being released. Ed, who'd been doing a stint for drug possession and bail jumping, apparently had not availed himself of the rehab programs offered by the prison. He just couldn't wait to get a buzz on, and when we say that, it's not just an expression of speech; he was so keen on getting blasted that he instructed the friends who were picking him up to bring some "goodies" with them. So keen he didn't exactly make the request quietly—prison authorities heard him do it.

A Delivery from the Drugstore

So up drives the van with Ed's friends and out pop the authorities, who search the van. Inside they find marijuana and methamphetamines, and something else—that the *van* was actually a lab.

Ladies and gentlemen, let us take a moment to salute Ed's friends, who not only did not question the wisdom of bringing illegal drugs right to the doorstep of a correctional facility but indeed thought nothing of bringing an entire illegal drug manufacturing concern along for the ride. That takes a certain special mix of chutzpah and cluelessness. They have our admiration, for what little good it will do them as they sit in their tiny little cells for their alleged crimes. As for Ed, he didn't even make it to the parking lot before he was arrested on new drug charges.

Next time, Ed: patience.

Source: Associated Press

* * *

WHOOPS! WHICH ME? ON TV?

A Cocoa, Florida, man was told by his friends that he had been featured on the television show *America's Most Wanted*. Nuh-uh, said the man, and to prove it, he called the local cops and asked them to investigate whether he was on the show. Well, the good news was he wasn't featured on the show. The bad news was that he was wanted for failure to appear in court regarding a battery with great bodily harm. The man was unaware of the warrant, but thanks to his call to the police, he found out about it pretty quick. He was arrested shortly thereafter.

Source: *Florida Today*

TIPS FOR STUPID CRIMINALS

Why? Because it fulfills our court-mandated community service, that's why.

TAX DODGE

Today's tip: Whenever possible, avoid crimes that lend themselves to cheap, bitter irony.

Would that "Josh" had availed himself of this tip. Josh had been the chairman of the Taxpayers Association of Middletown, a small town north of New York City. So presumably he could have been expected to know *something* about the U.S. Tax Code, at least in passing, and the penalties for fiddling around with said code. This does not appear to have kept Josh from trying his luck at deceiving the Internal Revenue Service during the years 1995 through 2000, including filing forms that declared him not to be a U.S. citizen. Sadly for Josh, the IRS did not fall for his sudden expatriation or other high jinks and hauled him into court on numerous charges of tax evasion and obstruction (and while in court, he managed to pull down a perjury charge, just for fun), where he was convicted on five counts by a jury of his tax-paying peers.

Ironic? Oh my, yes. Josh can't even claim ignorance as a defense. Just stupidity.

Source: *Middletown Times Herald-Record*

BEEKEEP, I'LL HAVE A STINGER

We're all for any legitimate therapeutic process that helps people kick a drug habit. Addiction is a real drag, and anything that you can do to stay off drugs is probably worth doing.

But, we're not so sure we'd follow the example of "Lee," a Chinese citizen who had been addicted to drugs since he left school over a decade earlier. Lee went to a variety of clinics, but he'd always resume his addictions once he got out the door.

Finally, he and his girlfriend headed for the mountains of Songpan County, away from the temptations of city life. But as anyone familiar with the crystal meth labs of rural Nebraska can tell you, just because you're in the middle of nowhere doesn't mean you can't find trouble.

Bee Happy

While on his mountain sabbatical, Lee read a magazine article about "apitherapy"—treating physical ailments with bee venom, fresh from the bee itself. Proponents of apitherapy tout it as a treatment for illnesses ranging from arthritis to asthma to heart disease. They also believe it can help drug users kick their habits.

This sounded good to Lee, but there were no available apitherapy clinics. However, since he was out in the country, there were a lot of bees. So Lee began a self-administered apitherapy regimen. Whenever he felt a craving for drugs, he'd seek out a hive of wild bees and let them sting him until his craving subsided.

To an outside observer this self-administered solution seems akin to ridding yourself of a toothache by feeding your hand to a badger. But Lee believed in it, and kept at it—for two years. That's a lot of bee stings. After two years, Lee claimed, he was cured of his addictions. One also suspects he'd developed something of an immunity to bee venom.

Lee eventually left his wild bees behind and now lives in the Chinese city of Chengdu, where he has a new job. He's a beekeeper. And why not?

Sources: *China Daily*, Ananova

* * *

FAILING BOTANY
Some teenagers in Ohio heard that, like, if you eat the seeds of the moonflower plant, you can totally get high! So 14 of them did. And shortly thereafter all 14 headed to the hospital with various symptoms including dilated pupils, rapid pulse, hallucinations, and an inability to urinate. Turns out "moonflower" plants (scientific name: *datura inoxia*) are toxic, which is something that they didn't hear from their stoner friends. Kids, just say no to eating random plants. Don't smoke banana peel either.

Source: Reuters

WHAT'S MORE, MIMING A BOMB THREAT ISN'T COOL, EITHER

They post the signs all over the place at the airport security stations: Do not make jokes about bombs. It's against the law, and it's a national law, so no matter where you go in the U.S., making a crack about a bomb is in fact a federal offense.

No cracking jokes. But what if you don't actually say the joke? What if you put a note into your suitcase, especially for the security guards? Surely those airport screeners would see the humor inherent in that maneuver, right? They'd just have a hearty chuckle, congratulate you for an innovative way to brighten their day, and wave you through.

The Trouble with Teens

Or not, as 17-year-old "Gil" from Paxton, Massachusetts, discovered in August 2003. He and his family were on a trip to Hawaii from Boston's Logan International Airport when security people found a happy little note note while pawing through his luggage. We now present it to you in all its expurgated wonder: "[Expletive] you. Stay the [expletive] out of my bag you [expletive] sucker. Have you found a [expletive] bomb yet? No, just clothes. Am I right? Yea, so [expletive] you."

The security people at Logan were so impressed with Gil's written communication that they felt they had to do something for him. And what they did was call the state police, who arrested Gil on the plane and ordered the rest of his family—Mom, Dad, and little sister—to get off the plane, too. (As this was all happening, according to the *Boston Globe*, Gil turned to his parents and said, in a classic teen comment, "I can explain this.") "Naturally, they searched his bag, and there was nothing else in the bag, but even if it was a prank, we take it very seriously," said Transportation Security Agency spokesperson Ann Davis.

So this year's fun-filled family trip wasn't to Hawaii after all, but to the East Boston District Court, where Gil pleaded not guilty to one count of making a bomb/hijacking threat, and was released on a $1,000 bond. That's money that probably would had gone to windsurfing lessons and a luau, had Gil just repressed his urge to be clever. Kids, there's a lesson there for you.

Sources: Associated Press, *Boston Globe*

* * *

FLY THE TOO-FRIENDLY SKIES

United Airlines ran a full-page ad in Denver newspapers advertising a special offer for rates along with a phone number to call. A call to that number provided another number for would-be customers to call. And that number was a phone sex line. Turns out that first heavily advertised number was incorrect. The number was also provided on flyers handed out at airports. "We apologize for any inconvenience this may have cost our customers," a United spokesperson said. Later flyers had the number blacked out.

Source: *Denver Post*

TIPS FOR STUPID CRIMINALS

That is, if they can read.

WHAT A FLOP!
Today's tip: When under house arrest, don't enter a
goofy sports contest covered by local media—
and certainly don't win one.

"George" was under house arrest—tellingly, for
violating his parole—when he got it in his
head to enter the belly-flop contest that is at
the heart (so to speak) of Red Belly Day in Fanning
Springs, Florida. Although weighing in at a mere 5'9"
and 182 pounds, George showed a certain special flair
for smacking hard on water and came away the contest
winner, a distinction that got his picture in the local
paper. Sadly for George, the local law enforcement saw
his picture in the paper and sent him up the river he
had so recently belly-flopped into, the better to serve a
three-year stint at the state prison in Lake Butler.

This meant that George was unable to defend his
title. "If I could get a furlough, I would be at that belly
flop contest this year," he said. Prison officials, perhaps
noting his previous inability to stay put, denied his furlough request.

Source: Associated Press

WHEN GAS SUPPLIES COME TO A DEAD STOP

Today's teenagers gape in disbelief when their grandparents tell them of the Great Gas Crisis of the 1970s—when people actually had to *wait in line* to buy gas, and sometimes even had to buy gas on *alternate days*! But if you want to hear a really interesting gas desperation story, try Zimbabwe in the summer of 2003. People weren't killing each other over gasoline, but dead people were being used to buy it.

Zimbabwe had been in a major gas crisis since November 2002, when a deal with Libya, which supplied about 70 percent of the nation's gas, got sunk. So naturally, rationing and long lines at the gas pump were the order of the day. But in one of those loopholes that just cried out for immoral exploitation, you could jump to the front of the gas line if your car was transporting a dead body to a funeral. All you needed was to a dead body.

He Doesn't Need to Fasten His Seatbelt

A Zimbabwean mortician and his assistant had an idea. For a fee, they'd give their gas-needing clients burial orders that made their cars hearses—and they'd also throw in a dead body (in a coffin, thankfully) as a rental. The client would hop to the front of the gas line, fill up, then drive back to the mortuary to return the coffin and the corpse. The mortician would get paid, the client would get the gas, and the corpse, presumably, wouldn't care one way or the other.

It worked for a while, but wouldn't you know, eventually the government had to come in and spoil the fun for everyone. The mortician and his assistant were both arrested and charged with violating dead bodies. They could have probably avoided this charge simply by renting out the coffins and not the actual corpses, because, honestly, the guy working at the gas station is not going to crack open a coffin to check.

Source: Reuters

* * *

INTERESTING WAY TO AVOID A PARKING TICKET

A man in Melbourne, Australia, was issued a parking ticket that he won't have to pay. The reason: he was dead at the time he got it. He was slumped over in the front seat of his car, motionless, when the parking officer came by and wrote up the ticket. She thought the guy was just sleeping. Eventually someone noticed the man was dead and called an ambulance. The parking officer, understandably distressed, was offered counseling.

Source: *Daily Telegraph*

THE REALLY STUPID QUIZ: THE WORLD OF FASHION

Strike a pose—it's time for another Really Stupid Quiz. Which of these is the genuine article and which are the cheap knockoffs? You decide.

1. Who let the dogs out—on the runway? While other musicians like Sean "P. Diddy" Combs are starting up clothing lines for people, a celebrity rapper/actor is tapping a heretofore underserved market: dogs. He announced the creation of a doggie-apparel line to debut in fall of 2003. The line will feature fashions specifically for the canine set, who to this point had been served primarily by homemade sweaters and ugly tartan saddles.

2. A well-known German fashion designer created a controversy when it was leaked that the models for his fall 2003 line, which he called "a commentary on the 'Heroin Chic' ideal in fashion" would feature drug addicts and recovering drug addicts recruited from private rehabilitation centers in Europe and the United States. In exchange for their services, he promised to pay for the cost of their treatments. The idea was later scrapped, although the designer suggested to the Austrian magazine *Profil* that he may return to the idea at some point.

3. A famous fashion designer announced that 2004 would see his company providing a new offering: high

heels for men. "We're tapping in to the whole 'metro-sexual' trend," said the designer's spokesperson, referring to the trend of straight male urbanites who enjoy things like facials and shopping. "We think that, cleverly done, the market is there." The first masculine high heels will feature relatively modest heels: two-and-a-half to three inches. "We recognize that we have to start from the ground up," the spokesperson said.

Which one is really stupid?

Answer page 311.

Sources: Ananova, *Rolling Stone*

* * *

YOUR CELEBRITIES AT WORK

"Gee honey, it's like being in a different country!"
—U.S. TV personality Kelly Ripa, to her husband, while in Montreal, Canada, to host a gala for the 2003 "Just For Laughs" comedy festival.

Source: *The Star*

DIAL "D" FOR DIVORCE

Thou shalt not commit adultery: not just a biblical commandment, but also a good idea. One reason—aside from the moral and philosophical issues surrounding the concept of fooling around with someone other than your spouse—is that it's easier to get caught than you might suspect. Not only that, but the world thinks up new and often exceptionally surprising ways to broadcast your infidelities to those who would be the most ticked off to learn about them.

"Nils," from Finland, found this out the hard way when he and his girlfriend decided to participate in some erotic calisthenics in his car. In the midst of their floor exercises, either Nils or his partner accidentally activated Nils's mobile phone and caused it to autodial a number. Who answered? Why, Nils's wife, of course. She picked up just in time to hear the mistress proclaim her love in the heat of passion. And wouldn't you know it, she recognized the mistress's voice as belonging to one of her so-called good friends.

Hitting Someone Is the Best Revenge

This led to Mrs. Nils marching over to her friend's apartment and punching her in the face, then going after Nils with an ax (he avoided injury). She was hauled into court and received a 14-month suspended sentence for the aforementioned attacks. Ultimately she and Nils ended up getting a divorce. Apparently she couldn't forgive the adultery and he couldn't forgive being mistaken for kindling.

Anyway, that's a lot of damage from one unintentional phone call. Keep that in mind the next time you're thinking of fooling around and have a cell phone nearby. One other warning: the newest cell phones can take pictures. All things considered, Nils is probably glad his couldn't.

Source: Reuters

* * *

CLOSE DOESN'T COUNT

A man wanted for murder almost got away from police with the use of a cell phone. When the car in which he was a passenger was pulled over by cops in South Bend, Indiana, the man in question pulled out his phone and made a quick call. Shortly thereafter, the cops who had pulled him over received a radio call that a gun-laden argument was going on in the lobby of the hotel across the street from where they were. The cops let the car go and entered the hotel lobby, which was quiet. The cops realized they'd been had, and tracked down the car a short distance away. The driver and wanted passenger were taken into custody. Nice try, though.

Source: *Indianapolis Star*

NOTE TO SELF:
911 DOESN'T TAKE REQUESTS

Maybe "Hal" was drinking and driving. Or maybe he just liked swerving down the road at high speeds. For whatever reason, our man Hal was rocketing down the road in Oklahoma and Texas, sometimes reaching speeds of more than 100 mph, trailing cop cars behind him like a string of Christmas lights tied to his bumper. All those cop cars on his tailpipe were getting on Hal's nerves.

So Hal decided to do something about it. He called 911. When the line for emergency services was picked up, Hal asked the dispatcher to call off the cop chase. Then he hung up and did it again. "I think he would just hit 9-1-1 and talk to whoever came on," said Oak Ridge police chief Clint Powell.

And it worked, sort of: the cops did stop chasing Hal. Not because he asked them to, but because they laid down road spikes outside of Powell, Oklahoma, which popped Hal's tires and made him stop. Hal was tossed into the clink on various vehicular charges and held on a $33,000 bond.

Let's hope his one phone call from jail was to another number.

Source: Associated Press

HISTORICAL DUMBOSITY: NOT-SO-GOLDEN OLDIE

Don't blame the 8-track for being dumb. It's not the 8-track's fault, really. All analog sound recording is a dead-end technology—LPs, cassette tapes, or reel-to-reel—it's all technologically dead compared to flawless and cheap digital technology, from CDs to MP3s. Even so, when you're looking for a combination of poor performance, questionable utility and—(click)—inherent technological limitations in any piece of technology, it's hard to beat an 8-track. Unlike so many unfortunate but promising technological cul-de-sacs, the 8-track is dead for a reason.

Petula Clark on Wheels

But let's be truthful. The 8-track was a piece of garbage, but it was pretty much designed to be that way. Most audio products are designed with at least some attempt toward sound quality. That wasn't the case with the 8-track, where the overriding idea was not quality but portability. The 8-track made its popular debut not in the middle of a swingin' '60s hi-fi rack, bracketed by *Playboys*, fondue makers, and Ian Fleming novels, but in a car. In 1965, the Ford Motor Company made the 8-track an option on all its 1966 models. The car was the 8-track's exclusive domain; there were no commercially available home units. The 8-track was available in an auto parts store instead of a record shop.

If you grant that the 8-track was designed with the road in mind, it's not an entirely unholy creation. In 1965 it was still well in the era of the AM radio and mono LP recording. Unless you wanted to play a harmonica and drive at the same time, there was no way to bring music *of your own choosing* into the car. Auto makers had actually tried putting record players into cars; it worked about as well as you might expect. In contrast, you could drive over train tracks and while your 8-track might warble a bit, it could nevertheless keep going. And it was stereo! Put *that* in your dashboard and play it!

The Lovin' Spoonful at Home

If the 8-track had stuck to the roads, where it was the best thing going, it might not have become a universal symbol of derision and pointlessness. But alas, it did not; 8-track players for the home came out in 1966, and there the format's shortcomings were exposed for all to see. Unlike reel-to-reel tape players, the sound reproduction of an 8-track was muddy, the effect of having eight tracks of music (four programs, a left and right channel each) on one half-inch strip of tape.

Unlike the LP, there was no ability to quickly go from one music track to another. Most 8-track players didn't bother with a fast forward or rewind option; you either had to know where all your favorite songs were in relation to each other in the programs and switch back and forth, or you had to sit there for the long haul and wait for them to come around again.

Even the compact cassette, which had worse

sound quality than the 8-track in the early days, had one up on the 8-tracks: no clicks. Because all four programs on an 8-track had to be of the same length, music listeners were often faced with either dead time at the end of a program or (even worse) the dreaded fade-out-click-and-fade-in phenomena, in which a song was butchered over two programs.

Pink Floydiana

This phenomenon however, made for some creative attempts to mask the click—in the 8-track version of Pink Floyd's *Animals* album, for example, there's a guitar solo, unavailable anywhere else, that acts as a bridge between "Pigs on the Wing" parts 1 and 2. It was done by Floyd tour guitarist Snowy White. Now you know something about Floyd that your terminally stoned, former college roommate didn't. Even better, he'll hate you for it. And they say there's no justice.

Mac Stops Thinking About Tomorrow

The 8-track was dying by the end of 1970s and was officially declared dead around 1983, when most major record companies stopped making them. After that date you had to get your 8-tracks from the record clubs, which manufactured the things until about 1989. If you look hard, you can actually find an 8-track of Michael Jackson's *Bad* album (but then, why would you). The last major album on 8-track, or so it is said, is Fleetwood Mac's *Greatest Hits*.

No one misses the 8-track, which is the final, incontrovertible proof of its dead ended-ness. Sure, people gawk in awe if you show up at a party with one, and if you somehow manage to get one to play, you'll be hailed as a hero of cheese. But this isn't the same as saying that anyone actually wants to hear music in the format anymore. Unlike old wax cylinders and 78-rpm Victrola records, there's nothing on 8-track that wasn't placed on a better recording medium as well. Unlike vinyl, you'll not hear of some geek audiophile haranguing bored listeners about the supposed sonic superiority of the 8-track.

Its only value today is to remind us that not every technological "advance" is a good one, or one that will last.

* * *

LIKE A DOOR WITH A
DEAD BOLT, LEFT WIDE OPEN

Maybe we're new to this, but we thought the whole reason the music industry wants to electronically copy-protect music CDs is to make it difficult to transfer the music from a CD to one's computer. This being the case, we're a little confused about the MediaMax CD3 copy protection, used by music giant BMG. The program automatically loads when you put it into your computer's drive, keeping you from copying the music to your hard drive. But in October 2003, a Princeton grad student found you could disable the software using this incredibly complicated procedure: hold down the "shift" key. Yes, really.

Yup, that'll stop the kids.

Source: C | Net.com

DUMB MOVIE FESTIVAL: *BATTLEFIELD EARTH* (2000)

Our Entry: *Battlefield Earth*, starring John Travolta and Forest Whitaker

The Plot (Such As It Is): Evil space aliens sporting dreadlocks enslave humanity and put them to work in various mines. One of the humans eventually rebels, an action that pits him and his fur-wearing partners against an alien named Terl (Travolta), who is most notable for looking like he mugged KISS bassist Gene Simmons and then got his makeup done on the Star Trek set. the movie is based on a really long novel of the same name by L. Ron Hubbard, founder of Scientology, of which Travolta is a member.

Fun Fact: Though it is generally acknowledged as one of the worst science fiction movies ever released by a major Hollywood studio, Travolta (who produced the film) is reportedly pleased with it and is considering attempting a sequel. Live that dream, John!

Total North American Box Office: $21,471,685 (source: The-Numbers.com). Not so good considering the $80 million production cost.

The Critics Rave!

"*Battlefield Earth* is just a lumbering, poorly photographed piece of derivative sci-fi drivel, full of grunting extras scampering around in animal pelts and more dank, trash-strewn sets than I ever care to see again."—*Entertainment Weekly*

"Even if you were to classify it as a guilty pleasure, it would be the kind of sullying guilt that makes people leap from heights."—*Portland Oregonian*

"So ineptly written, directed, acted and photographed it seems as if it were made by circus chimps . . . easily Travolta's worst movie ever, and that's saying something for a resumé that includes such atomic bombs as *Moment by Moment* and *Staying Alive*."—*Toronto Star*

"*Battlefield Earth* is like taking a bus trip with someone who has needed a bath for a long time. It's not merely bad; it's unpleasant in a hostile way."—*Chicago Sun-Times*

"Sitting through it is like watching the most expensively mounted high school play of all time . . . [The film] is beyond conventional criticism. It belongs in the elect pantheon that includes such delights as *Showgirls* and *Revolution*: the Moe Howard School of Melodrama."
—*New York Times*

"Sitting through the summer's first monolithic monstrosity, *Battlefield Earth*, was one of the most painfully excruciating experiences of my life. This film . . . is the *Plan 9 from Outer Space* of the new millennium. It's the film that the infamous Edward D. Wood, Jr., might have made if he had been handed $100 million. Actually, Ed Wood would have done a better job."—*Sacramento Bee*

LIKE A RAT IN A DAZE

I f you have a rat or a mouse scooting around in the attic, you might think you have an infestation. Well, not to take anything away from your rodent problem, but it's nothing compared to what has been going on at the police station in Caboolture, a town north of Brisbane in Australia.

The place is crawling with rats, which is bad enough. But some of the rats apparently got into the evidence room, and started snacking on what they found there—bags filled with pot and speed.

Just Say No to Evidence

Queensland Police Union general secretary Phil Hocken described the rats, "their eyes wide open, running frantically for no reason at all, round in circles." The rats were on a rampage in the station ceiling, scampering back and forth like windup toys. As a delightful aside, rat pee was reported dripping down the walls.

And, on an entirely incidental but significant jurisprudential note, imagine being the prosecuting lawyer in a drug case, trying not to get your case thrown out of court because the evidence was ingested by rodents. Caboolture police have responded to the problem by storing drug evidence in sealed containers and laying traps to catch the drug-addled rats. For bait, might we suggest pizza and snack cakes. Sooner or later, those rats are going to get a serious case of the munchies.

Source: *Queensland Daily Mail*

TIPS FOR STUPID CRIMINALS

*You can tell which ones they are because they move their
lips while they're reading this book.*

JAIL BREAK
Today's tip: When escaping jail through an open
window, make sure the width of your body does not
exceed that of the window.

In June 2003, inmate #456789 decided he'd had
enough of Elkhart County Jail hospitality. But,
seeing as he was in a jail cell and all, he wasn't
exactly able to walk out through the front door. So he
attempted an exit through the window of his jail cell
and managed to get just enough of himself through the
window to become well and truly trapped; it took the
fire department to dislodge him.

Funny thing is, he *did* manage to get out of jail by
going through the window—but that's only because he
was then sent to the hospital, under guard, to be
treated for lacerations he got trying to cram himself
through the window.

* * *

"Not so much brain as ear wax."
—**William Shakespeare**

DEAR GOD: NEXT TIME
SEND AN E-MAIL

T he problem with asking for a sign from God is that sometimes you get one. Just ask the congregation of the First Baptist Church in Forest, Ohio. At the beginning of July the church was filled with devout Christians listening to a guest pastor preach on the subject of penance when a storm began brewing outside. As part of the guest pastor's sermon, he asked God to give them all a sign that he was listening.

"You could hear the storm building outside . . . He (the pastor) just kept asking God what else he needed to say," church member Ronnie Cheney said to a reporter afterward. "He was asking for a sign!"

And wouldn't you know. At just that moment, a bolt of lighting coursed down from the sky, zapped the church steeple, and then plunged into the church electrical system, exiting by way of the microphone the preacher was using. Churchgoers reported that the minister was briefly swaddled in electrical bolts before the charge dissipated, blowing out the church's sound system in the process.

On with the Show

Miraculously, the minister was unhurt. Not only unhurt, but like any good showman, he was ready to roll with this bit of divine improvisation. He continued his service for another 20 minutes before another sign manifested itself: the church was in flames.

Congregants took this as a sign to get the heck out of the church and call the fire department; the building sustained an estimated $20,000 in damage.

Now, it could have been coincidence. And maybe from a theological point of view it would be better to think about it that way.

After all, when you're being lectured on penance and someone asks for a sign from God and He responds with 300 million volts and $20,000 in damages, what does that say?

Source: Associated Press

* * *

SAFE-TY FIRST

He was dared by the other Wooster, Ohio, K-Mart employees to see if he could fit into the four-by-two-foot safe. So, like any 18-year-old with more flexibility than brains, he pretzeled himself into the safe, which his coworker closed once he was in. And which (of course) couldn't open up again, undoubtedly causing his enclosed friend to wonder just how much oxygen was inside a teen-stuffed closed safe. It took a visit from the firemen to get him out. So if someone dares you to crawl into one of the things, play it safe. Yes, pun intended.

Source: Newsday.com

THE REALLY STUPID QUIZ: STUPIDITY AT WORK

Time to punch in for our final Really Stupid Quiz! One of these subjects deserves a promotion; two need to be laid off. You make the call.

1. A midlevel manager at a Pittsburgh office found himself standing in the unemployment line because of a leaked memo in which he spoke of employees slated to be laid off in mafioso-like terms, describing them as "capped" and "sleeping with the fishes." The manager had written the memo at the request of his own supervisors and left it, in e-mail form, on his computer while he attended a meeting. In his absence, someone entered his office, saw the memo and e-mailed it to the employees slated to be laid off; from there the e-mail was forwarded on to others. The manager was first suspended and then fired by the company, which cited the manager's "insensitivity with an especially sensitive issue." The company also offered an apology to the workers on the list, but refused to comment on whether those employees would be spared a layoff.

2. A Dutch funeral home worker was fired after he lost a coffin, with a body inside, on the way to a funeral. The worker in question was in a hearse, driving the coffin to its final resting place, when the back of the hearse opened and the coffin fell out on the road. Oblivious to the situation, the worker drove on; a short while later a bus pulled alongside the hearse

and the agitated bus driver told the worker he'd left his payload down the street. "I thought he made a joke," said the puzzled funeral home worker. "But when I went back I saw it was indeed my coffin." The funeral home canned the worker, citing his lack of respect for the dead.

3. An owner of a Haitian textile factory is recovering from injuries sustained while attempting to convince his workers that the factory was not cursed. Workers at the factory reported that the mother of a former coworker paid to have a curse placed on the factory by a voodoo priest because she felt her son had been wrongly fired. A number of workers refused to enter the factory afterward, so the owner invited them to follow him around the factory. As the owner walked down stairs to the factory floor, he tripped and fell, fracturing an arm and his jaw and suffering a gash to his temple that required several stitches. While still maintaining there was no curse, the owner offered to pay a voodoo priest to lift the curse so his workers would feel comfortable returning to work.

Which one is really stupid?

Answer page 311.

Source: Ananova

NOW FOR THE
IN-FLIGHT ENTERTAINMENT

S treaking—running about in a public place sans
clothing—is not something we recommend that
you do. The whole point of streaking is to make
people look, and far too many of us have let ourselves get
to the point where when we're naked, people want to
look away, which defeats the whole purpose.

But if you must streak, here are some ground rules:

First, have an escape route.

Second, don't streak somewhere you're going to
have to explain yourself later.

Third, leave 'em wanting more. Nothing's worse
than a streaker who has overstayed his welcome.

"Sid" managed to break all three of these ground
rules—with unfortunate results. The place he chose for
his streak was the aisle of a Singapore Airlines airplane, on a flight between Perth, Australia, and
Singapore. As you may know, airplanes in midflight are
notoriously stingy with paths for egress. And coincidentally, Sid's day job was as a flight steward for
Singapore Airlines. At the time, he was off duty, but
he was still on company grounds. And you can bet if
he doesn't lose his job over this one, it's going to make
some awkward moments with his coworkers.

He Didn't Even Give Us Peanuts

Finally, and not to put too fine a point on it, Sid went
a little bonkers while he was running around naked.
First he splashed wine on other passengers, then he

began prancing through the aisles. "He wasn't even wearing underwear. He was shouting, and tossing credit cards and photos out of his wallet all over the plane," a passenger told the *Straits Times* newspaper of Singapore.

It was a heck of a show, but all shows have to come to an end, and after a bit of hide and seek with the cabin staff (whose path to Sid was blocked by food carts. Ha! Now they know what it's like!), they managed to grab him, cover him with blankets and convince him that it wasn't a clothes-optional flight. Shortly after the flight landed in Singapore, Sid was hustled off to the hospital. See—he should have planned that escape route a little more carefully.

Sources: *Straits Times*, Reuters

* * *

GIVE THIS GUY A CELL PHONE

What happens when an FBI agent loses his gun at a major U.S. airport? Now we know. In October 2003, an FBI agent at Denver Airport misplaced his traveling bag, complete with gun and credentials, while he took a phone call. After he realized he'd lost the bag, the entire B concourse of the airport was shut down for 30 minutes while they searched for it. This delayed a dozen flights and kept passengers from entering and leaving the concourse. They eventually found the bag in the restaurant where the agent ate earlier. Well, of course. Stuff like that's always in the last place you look.

Source: Associated Press

TIPS FOR STUPID CRIMINALS

*Because just when you think they couldn't get any
stupider, really, they do.*

ARMED AND NOT DANGEROUS
Today's tip: Your finger is not a gun.

We shouldn't have to point this one out, but apparently we do. In June 2003, "Seth" walked into a pharmacy in Neillsville, Wisconsin, with a mask on, made a thumb-and-finger gun with one gloved hand, and tried to convince the pharmacist that he was about to be robbed. Unfortunately for Seth, what the pharmacist thought was going on was that some profoundly delusional nutcase in a mask was making an ass of himself in his store.

The pharmacist came out from behind the counter, wrestled Seth to the ground, and ripped off his mask. Seth managed to skulk away but was arrested by the police shortly thereafter. It should be noted that Seth did not try his finger gun maneuver on the cops when they came to get him.

So there's still hope for Seth. Not *much*, just a little.

Sources: Associated Press, The Smoking Gun

DUI DOUBLE TROUBLE

We don't really have anything against the drunk and foolish, but we do think, as a rule, that they shouldn't be allowed to operate machinery that moves from place to place. Furthermore, we strongly believe that those of us in charge of keeping the drunk and foolish off the road (i.e., police) should probably err on the side of caution when assessing the ability of the drunk and foolish to be mobile.

Our belief in this is only reinforced by this story, from the far northern country of Norway, in which officers came across a woman weaving over the roads one night. Our officers apprehended the woman, who cheerfully admitted to being drunk—and with a blood alcohol count of 1.7, "drunk" is a polite way of putting it. They took her down to the station, confiscated her license, and then (this being Norway, we guess), released her.

All Boozed Up and No Place to Go

Apparently, her place of residence was not ready for occupancy, so she asked if she could "crash" in her car. The police, taking pity on her, gave her back her keys—but they also disconnected the ignition distributor of her car, figuring that would keep her in one place until she could sleep it off.

Silly, trusting, naive Norwegian police. Several hours later the cops spotted someone weaving drunkenly down the road, and who should it be but, you guessed it, our sleepy-headed drunken gal. This time, she was stopped with a big ol' bottle of beer between her knees and a blood alcohol level of 1.8—even higher than the first time she was stopped. The woman was drunk, but she was not so drunk she couldn't reconnect the wires to her distributor and haul ass down the road. Our lesson: don't trust the drunken and foolish, or you'll end up looking foolish yourself.

This second time, we assume (and pray), they gave her someplace to sleep inside the police station. Hopefully with some bars. And without the keys.

Sources: *Bergens Tidende, Aftenposten*

* * *

SKUNKED!

Sure, playing with roadkill may seem like a good idea. But here's why it's not. Four Massachusetts teens ended up getting rabies shots after three of them decided to pull a prank on a fourth, and dragged a dead skunk into their pal's car. After they all had a good laugh, they chucked the skunk's corpse back into the woods. It was all fun and games until someone remembered skunks can carry rabies, and the police were dispatched to retrieve the skunk for testing. The body was too decomposed for accurate testing, and you know what that means: shots for everyone! (Well, except for the skunk.) So, kids, leave the roadkill alone. It's just that many fewer injections down the road.

Source: The Boston Channel.com

DUMB, FOR GOODNESS' SAKE

As much fun as it is to mock those who do stupid things, every once in a while someone does something dumb for understandable— nay, even *noble*—reasons. Such a person is "Nigel," a mail carrier from Gloucester, England.

Nigel's crime was discovered when the tenant of one of Nigel's rental properties went up into the attic of his home and found massive piles of mail stored there. Further investigation disclosed that it wasn't just any kind of mail. It was the most dreaded of all mail— no, not your bills—*junk* mail.

Nearly 4,000 pieces of junk mail, to be precise.

The Mail Must Not Go Through

Confronted with the incriminating evidence, Nigel confessed to storing the junk mail, opening some to confirm it was indeed junk mail, and even burning some of it (for which he was duly charged with stealing, opening, and burning mail). But he had a good reason. He said that due to the volume of junk mail he had to deliver, he simply couldn't deliver it all on time; his mailbag was just too heavy for him to haul around. So he sorted out all the junk mail, stowed it in the attic, and delivered the rest of the mail instead.

"He believed he could deliver the letters later, but then he reached the point of no return," said Nigel's solicitor. "He found the burden of dealing with so much junk mail too much to bear."

Well, and who could blame him? It's bad enough

getting it. One suspects if they polled the people on Nigel's route as to whether or not they really missed all the junk mail, they might have decided that instead of firing Nigel (which they did), they ought to give him a medal instead. But for all that, even well-intentioned junk-mail theft is mail theft, and Nigel could very well be stamped undeliverable while he spends some time behind bars.

Source: *Gloucester Echo*

* * *

THEY NEVER HAD A CHANCE!
In October 2003, Californians chose superstar Arnold Schwarzenegger to be their new governor in a special recall election, out of a field of more than 130 candidates. Schwarzenegger reeled in almost 3,750,000 votes. But you ask: how did diminutive former child star and fellow candidate Gary Coleman do? Here are his numbers and those of some other "notables":

Gary Coleman: 12,690 votes
Larry Flynt (Hustler publisher): 15,464
Mary "Mary Carey" Cook (adult film actress): 10,114
Gallagher (comedian): 4,864
Angelyne (professional blonde): 2,262

The lowest vote getter? West Hollywood businessman Todd Lewis, with 172.

Source: CNN

TIPS FOR STUPID CRIMINALS

Because we like to see them get all indignant about the fact that we think they're stupid.

EXCUSE ME, BUT DO YOU KNOW WHERE I CAN BUY A GUN?
Today's tip: Don't tell strangers that you've just escaped from prison.

I nmate "Ben" planned his escape from the Nebraska State Penitentiary meticulously. Having just been sentenced to 18 to 22 years for robbery, Ben managed to get hold of handcuff keys and made a daring escape from the prison parking lot as he was being transferred into the big house. After springing himself from the cuffs, he raced through the parking lot to a car planted there by friends. The car had keys in the ignition and a change of clothes. Off he sped to freedom, or what passes for freedom when you're the object of an intensive statewide manhunt.

So high marks to Ben for the initial escape. But of course this makes the next thing he did even more incomprehensible. After four days of successfully eluding police, Ben marched up to two complete strangers on a street in Lincoln, Nebraska, and asked them if they could help him get a gun, since he was a recent escapee from prison. The only possible explanation for this sort of behavior is that perhaps Ben thought that, being a minor local celebrity—what with his picture in the paper and all—complete strangers would be so dazzled by his roguish persona that they would be willing to risk a little prison time themselves to help an escaped felon secure a lethal weapon.

However, in this case, the strangers were not impressed with Ben's claim to fame and asked him to prove it. Ben wandered off to find a newspaper with his name and picture in it. Meanwhile, our total strangers, motivated no doubt by the desire to remove a dangerous criminal from the streets (and also to partake of the $2,500 reward that was being offered for information leading to Ben's arrest) took advantage of his absence to call the local law enforcement. When Ben returned, the boys in blue bagged him and hauled him away.

The obligatory comment from law enforcement regarding the intelligence of the criminal, via Lt. Mark Funkhauser of the Nebraska State Patrol: "We're not dealing with Harry Houdini here." No, indeed.

Source: *Omaha World-Herald*

* * *

OOPS, I DID IT AGAIN

Pop diva Britney Spears might want to watch her step in Maryland: the state's first lady is gunning for her. Kendel Ehrlich, wife of Governor Robert Ehrlich, was commenting on Spears's apparently less-than-savory influence on American youth when she opined "Really, if I had an opportunity to shoot Britney Spears, I think I would." She was at a conference on domestic violence. Did Mrs. Ehrlich release a press statement the next day, sheepishly acknowledging she would not, in fact, hit Britney, baby, one more time? Oh, my, yes.

Source: STLToday.com

ANOTHER ONE FOR THE "EXPECTING TOO MUCH FROM FERMENTED POTATOES" FILE

I n the first half of 2003, everyone was a little spooked by the SARS virus. It was like a common cold genetically spliced with the Terminator, and for a while there it seemed like you could get it simply by thinking about it. Since China appeared to be the epicenter of the contagion, a number of people looked at citizens of that country as potential carriers.

This explains why six Russian men in Blagoveshchensk were twitchy about the Chinese workers at a nearby construction site. Our heroes assumed that the Chinese workers were Far East versions of Typhoid Mary, just waiting to slip the dreaded SARS past their delicate Russian immunological systems. But our Russians a had a plan. They had heard Russian scientists say that vodka could ward off the SARS virus. And by golly, they were going to get themselves immunized as soon as possible.

A Vodka Tonic

The funny thing is, this wasn't just one of those hopeful Russian folktales about the healing power of vodka, another on the list of the potent potable's many magical qualities. Russian scientists really *did* suggest a belt of vodka to ward off SARS. According to the Ananova news service, researchers at Moscow's Medical Academy suggested in May 2003 that 10 centiliters of vodka (that's a double shot) administered daily, should be more than enough to keep the virus at bay. This is on top of vodka's other medically significant qualities, such as making you smarter, wittier, stronger, and more attractive.

The problem for our six Russian friends was that while they did, in fact, self-administer the suggested daily double shot, they drank a little more as well, just to be sure SARS couldn't get the slightest toehold. A week later, after constant self-medication, our boys landed in the hospital with severe alcohol poisoning, from which they would take a week to recover. So while they didn't have SARS, they got to feel almost as bad as if they had.

Remember: vodka—use only as directed.

Source: Ananova

* * *

SMOKIN' AND DRINKIN'

Cities and states across the United States are banning smoking in bars. But in south Florida, one bar is ready for smokers who don't want to leave the bar for their nicotine fix: the nicotini. The *South Florida Sun-Sentinel* reported that Larry Wald, the owner of the Cathode Ray Club, invented the drink by soaking tobacco leaves in vodka. The drink, which costs anywhere between $3 for a shot and $5.50 for a cocktail, is also available in menthol and in a Kahlua-flavored version known as the "Black Lung." Drink up!

Source: *South Florida Sun-Sentinel*

THE REALLY STUPID QUIZ: THE ROCKY ROAD TO LOVE

Say "I Do" to another Really Stupid Quiz! One of these is the real deal; two of these should be left at the altar. Which is which?

1. A wedding in Odessa, Texas, was abruptly canceled midceremony after the bridegroom attempted to change the wedding vows without his bride's permission. The bride, Cynthia Gates, had removed the admonition "to obey" from the vows, but groom Charles Curtis secretly asked the minister to reinsert it. "When she heard 'obey' her eyes got real wide, her face turned red, and she started yelling at Chuck," the maid of honor said. "It was a mess." Gates took the wedding limousine to the apartment the couple shared, and threw Curtis's belongings into the street. Police later called to the scene by Curtis refused to intervene. "She's the lease holder," an officer at the scene said. "She has the right to kick him out."

2. An Iraqi man is getting married with a little help from deposed dictator Saddam Hussein. When the city of Baghdad fell to U.S. forces, our man entered one of Hussein's palaces and helped himself to one of the beds he found there. The bed, made of mahogany, was so large that it took the man four trips to carry it to his home across the street. His fiancée was so impressed with the bed that she agreed to marry him. "I'm very happy," he said. "Fate has finally been

good to me and Saddam's bed has helped me become a better man." He also took a pair of slippers and an end table.

3. An Australian man's wedding proposal went seriously awry. Joe Griggs of Brisbane had convinced the owner of a highway billboard near his home to let him put up a temporary sign asking his girlfriend Nicole Hathaway to marry him. Once it was up, Griggs took Hathaway for a drive and as the car passed the sign, Griggs pointed it out to her. Hathaway was so overcome by the sign that she tried to hug Griggs; in the process Griggs lost control of his car and struck a highway sign. The impact inflated the driver's-side air bag, breaking Griggs's nose. The two were otherwise unhurt, but the car was "smashed beyond repair." The good news: Hathaway said yes.

Which one is really stupid?

Answer page 311.

Source: Ananova

* * *

"The good Lord set definite limits on man's wisdom, but set no limits on his stupidity—and that's just not fair."

—**Konrad Adenauer**

DUMB MOVIE FESTIVAL: *DUNGEONS & DRAGONS* (2000)

Our Entry: *Dungeons & Dragons*, starring Jeremy Irons and Thora Birch

The Plot (Such As It Is): Jeremy Irons runs around chewing scenery and wielding a magic rod (heh) to command dragons and steal a kingdom from the teenage queen (Thora Birch). Somehow—the details are fuzzy—three WB-like postteens become involved and have many adventures that look like they were filmed on the set of *Xena: Warrior Princess* while that crew was at lunch. Eventually there's a battle scene with dragons that doesn't make much sense, much to the disappointment of every D&D geek in the world.

Fun Fact: *D&D* director Courtney Solomon bought the rights to make the *D&D* movie when he was a wee lad of twenty and spent the next 10 years trying to find financing for it. Somewhere in that decade, a couple of correspondence film courses might have been nice, Mr. Solomon.

Total North American Box Office: $15,185,241 (source: The-Numbers.com). The good news for New Line Cinema (which distributed the film in the U.S.) is they got that whole fantasy thing right just in time for the *Lord of the Rings* movies.

The Critics Rave!

"A misbegotten exercise in abject incompetence . . . produces all the magic and fun of a slow root canal. It features heroes you despise, dangers you giggle at, and dialogue that beggars belief. Insiders will look at this movie and cringe in horror."
—Flipside Movie Emporium

"As the evil Profion, one of an elite race of magic users called Mages, Irons is nearly incomprehensible from his first line to his last . . . but it's also likely that he's not even speaking English, since much of his dialogue consists of mumbled incantations along the lines of "gabba gabba hey." The rest of the time, when he's not laughing maniacally ("bwaa-HA-HA-HA!"), you can't make him out because his mouth is so full of scenery he makes Gilbert Gottfried look like Sir Laurence Olivier."—*Washington Post*

"Any dungeon master worth his 20-sided dice could have whipped up a better scenario."—*Northwest Herald* (Crystal Lake, IL)

"*Dungeons & Dragons* looks like they threw away the game and photographed the box it came in . . . The plot does not defy description, but it discourages it."—*Chicago Sun-Times*

"It's astonishing to see a film in which every single actor manages to embarrass him or herself with such regularity."
—Daily-Reviews.com

"Even with your +2 Ring of Histrionic Resistance, you're hosed. For the rest of the movie, you will suffer the effects of some of the worst acting in recent memory."—*Edmonton Sun*

"The clumsiest, most inept cinematic exploitation of an item with kid appeal that we have yet seen."—*Detroit News*

PSYCHED OUT

P sychology is a fascinating field, but when it comes to performing psychological experiments on unsuspecting Joes on the street, it's probably better to leave it up to Stanley Milgram and his merry band of hand-zappers. This is the lesson three University of Connecticut students learned in May 2003, when their own unauthorized psychological experiment produced interesting and unexpected results: namely, the three of them getting hauled away to the hoosegow.

Experiment in Error

It all started when "Tim," "Sam," and "Ann" staged a brilliant and original mock kidnapping near UConn's West Hartford campus. Passers-by were treated to the sight of a person, bound and gagged, sitting in the backseat of a car. The tied-up person was then forced out of the car by two "assailants," who then threatened the "victim"; the victim then approached the undoubt-edly horrified spectators, asking them what, if any-thing, they were going to do. One of them called the police, who later spotted the car on campus.

One thing led to another, and before long the police were administering a psychological experiment of their own to our trio of terrors: studying how dimwitted students react when hauled down to the precinct. "I think they actually yanked them out of finals," said Detective Capt. Bill Erickson of the West Hartford police. "They may get an incomplete."

Dumb Students Deserve Jail

Spokespeople for the University of Connecticut's psychology department were not notably sympathetic to the plight of the three students, in part because all student experiments are supposed to be cleared by the department for certain ethical standards, one of which probably includes keeping them out of the reach of the long arm of the law. "If students want to go out and do jackass stunts on their own, they probably should be arrested," said David Miller, associate head of UConn's psychology department.

Source: Associated Press

* * *

YOU'VE GOT MAIL. LOTS OF MAIL.

In the old days, students might prank a teacher with a tack on the chair or maybe a phone call in the middle of the night. But today's children are industrious—and they have access to the Internet. Which is why, we suppose, the 15-year-old boy from Singapore decided to prank his teacher by sending not one, not two, but 161,064 e-mail messages. You know. Just in case she deleted the first couple of thousand. At the kid's hearing, his defender noted that he was trying to "increase his self-esteem and ego," by spamming his teacher. This rationale would explain a lot about spammers in general.

Source: *Sydney Morning Herald*

FOR GERBIL'S SAKE!

We can think of a lot of good reasons not to do methamphetamines. First and most obviously, they're illegal, which means by doing them, you risk ending up in a tiny concrete room with nothing to do for a couple of years but watch *Jerry Springer* on a TV locked behind a grate. Not really a pleasant prospect for most people.

Another reason is that methamphetamines have a nasty list of side effects, like nausea, tremors, dizziness, hyperthermia, heart failure, and stroke—many of which can land on your plate all at once, like a hellish smorgasbord. And if you use too much of the stuff, it starts playing with your head, causing a delightful condition that's known as toxic psychosis, which makes you all paranoid and twitchy. Yeah, *that* sounds like fun.

Of course, people who are pharmaceutically paranoid end up doing some pretty bizarre things. Take "Theo" from Ventura County, California, who was sentenced to 50 days in jail for actions stemming from his methamphetamine use.

The Furry Friend
Theo's problem was that the meth made him think that someone living in his house was a spy for the government. Someone small. Someone innocent. Someone . . . fuzzy. Specifically, his daughter's gerbil.

How on earth could a gerbil be a government spy, you ask? Well, you're just asking that because you're *not* all hopped up on intense, brain-chemistry-changing stimulants. When you *are*, it makes perfect sense. It made sense to Theo. He even discussed his reasoning with the neighbors: the gerbil's teeth were bar coded, he confided. There was a camera in its little furry head. At this point we imagine the neighbors smiling politely, going back to their house and telling their kids to run fast in the other direction whenever Theo came out of the house.

What happened with the gerbil we won't describe in detail, except you may rest assured that it did not end well for our unfortunate little furry operative. Theo was convicted for cruelty to animals and being under the influence of methamphetamines. In addition to 50 days in jail, he was also ordered to psychological testing and drug counseling.

Here's the lesson: just say no.

If you can't do it for yourself, do it for the gerbils.

Sources: Associated Press, goaskalice.columbia.edu

* * *

"He was born stupid, and greatly increased his birthright."

—**Nicholas Murray Butler**

TIPS FOR STUPID CRIMINALS

Think of these as good deeds for bad people.

DON'T GET CAUGHT WITH
YOUR HAND IN THE TILL
Today's tip: The object of robbing a store is to
make money, not lose it.

Gary's plan to rob a store in Ayr, Scotland, was
simple. Go in, buy a pack of cigarettes with a
£10 note, and while the register is open, reach
in and swipe the contents. It was a foolproof plan.

But what happened next just goes to show that
most "foolproof" plans just haven't met the right fool.
Gary executed the first part of his plan to perfection,
asking for the cigarettes and producing the £10 note
to "pay" for them. So far, so good. He then produced
a hammer and threatened the shopkeeper with it.
Disappointingly, she wasn't notably threatened and
told him where he and his hammer could go.

Nevertheless, she'd opened the register. Gary the
intrepid robber then swooped down to scoop out the
contents. The shopkeeper slammed the till on his
fingers. Through the pain, Gary grabbed a few bills and
sprinted out the door, leaving his cigarettes and his £10
note behind. When the shopkeeper counted her losses,
she discovered the robber had grabbed only £5, mean-
ing he'd lost £5 in the whole felonious transaction.

What do you know—crime really *doesn't* pay.

Source: *Daily Record* (U.K.)

THAT'S ONE LUCKY MAN

So, how much spending money does one human being need on him at any one time? If you're an average person, you can probably get by with a hundred bucks or so, maybe a little more if you're planning a big night on the town and need to tip the waiters and the pole dancers.

Don't believe us? Ask Jack Whittaker, who won the Powerball lottery in 2002, netting himself a tidy $170 million lump sum (before taxes). So this isn't a fellow who has to worry about a dropped $20 bill here and there. But even Mr. Whittaker had cause for alarm when someone broke into his SUV and made off with a bit of cash he had in a briefcase in the passenger seat. It wasn't much. Just $545,000. Well, to be fair, it wasn't actually a half million in cash. About half was in the form of cashier's checks.

Dumb, But Lucky
And what, you ask, did Whittaker need with all that cash? Well, he was at a strip joint when it happened. And he has a reputation for tipping well. But probably not that well. Police said that Whittaker was probably bound for a game of chance—and why wouldn't he be? He was a man lucky enough to have won $170 million. The residue of that luck pulled him through this time —the money that had been plucked from his SUV was found not far away in some bushes. All of it. That's like winning the lottery twice.

Just in case you're wondering, the police nabbed

two suspects—the strip club manager and his gal pal, who allegedly drugged Whittaker and then snuck out and grabbed the cash. How did they know it was there? The gal pal saw him take some money out of the brief-case earlier in the evening. Whittaker's definitely the victim here, but come on—he did everything but put a "MONEY HERE" neon sign over his wad o' cash.

Mr. Whittaker doesn't need out advice, but just in case: dude—credit cards exist for a reason. And you criminals? Next time, put those ill-gotten gains *away* somewhere!

Sources: *Charleston* (WV) *Daily Mail*, Associated Press

* * *

"Only the wisest and stupidest of men never change."
—**Confucius**

"You have to believe in God before you can say there are things that man was not meant to know. I don't think there's anything man wasn't meant to know. There are just some stupid things that people shouldn't do."
—**David Cronenberg**

HISTORICAL DUMBOSITY: ANOTHER MEGALOMANIAC HAS A GO AT IT

We've already seen how Napolean's army failed to conquer Russia . . . Maybe someone else would have more luck?
(Part I is on page 243.)

Fast forward a century or so to 1941. Hitler had been playing nice with Russia (the Soviet Union) while German troops rampaged through the rest of Europe. But finally he decided it was time to try his luck to the east in a campaign known as Barbarossa).

For this campaign, Hitler assembled a force that made Napoleon's Grand Army look like a marching band: 150 army divisions with a total of 3 million men, 3,000 tanks, 7,500 artillery, and 2,500 airplanes. Thrown in almost as an afterthought were another 30 divisions of Finnish and Romanian troops. On June 22, 1941, this force attacked on three wide fronts, overwhelming the underpowered Soviet army. Hitler and his crew confidently estimated that in no more than six months, the battles would be over because of lack of support from the Soviet citizens.

What a Dummkopf!

Hitler and the Germans might not have learned the lessons of 1812, but the Soviets sure did, particularly the "scorched earth" policy that starved Napoleon's troops as they marched toward Moscow. The Soviets torched their crops, destroyed bridges, moved factories to the Russian interior, and moved or junked railroad engines and cars, leaving little behind for the Germans to use for their own advantage. In spite of this, the Germans initially made some excellent progress: by mid-July they were closing in on Moscow and had done pretty nicely on their other fronts as well.

But then things began to break down. Back in Germany, Hitler and his generals squabbled about what to do next, which slowed the advance of the German army.

That Weather Thing Again

Wild weather in July turned much of Russia into a mud pit, making it difficult for German vehicles to move. The Soviet army, which was supposed have gone kaplooey, kept stubbornly bringing up more troops—far more than the Germans had planned to fight. And as the year got older, the weather got worse.

In October, the Germans were on the doorstep of Moscow, close enough to *taste it*, when one of the coldest winters on record just stomped right in and proceeded to taunt the shivering Germans. Tanks, planes, and artillery froze—and so did the German soldiers, whose clothing was ill-equipped for the Russian winter's subzero temperatures. And no one makes winter like Mother Russia makes winter. (Her special ingredient is frostbite!)

You Call That Cold?

The Soviet army, on the other hand, was used to the cold, and didn't mind pressing its advantage. By November 1941, the Germans had suffered some

730,000 casualties. The Germans were now well inside the Russian black hole and would stay there, sapping Germany's military strength. This was, of course, much to the advantage of Great Britain (which had been close to the breaking point before Hitler invaded Russia) and the other Allies in the west, including the United States.

We like to think the United States won the war, but it was in Russia where Germany's collapse was born. Don't think the Germans didn't know it, either—at the end of the war they prayed that the U.S. and British troops would get to Berlin before the Soviets did, and Hitler's successor Karl Dönitz spent most of his short reign trying to get as many German civilians and troops into U.S. and British hands before the Soviets came calling (in retrospect, not a bad idea). We did our part, but it was Russia that bled Nazi Germany dry.

So don't be dumb, O Emperor (or Empress) of Europe! Stay out of Russia. Your empire will thank you. And so will the Russians.

* * *

"Those who know, and know that they know, are wise. You may follow them. Those who know not, and know they know not, are smart. You can teach them. Those who know not, and know not that they know not, are dumb. You must leave them."
—**Native American Proverb**

THE ANSWER ZONE

Below are answers to the "Really Stupid Quizzes."

1. Escaped Prisoners (page 29)
Answer: #2

2. Wacky World Leaders (page 39)
Answer: #1

3. Artsy-Fartsy (page 68)
Answer: #3

4. Sensitivity (page 191)
Answer: #3

5. Those Crazy Teens! (page 202)
Answer: #1

6. Those Disturbing Animals! (page 224)
Answer: #3

7. Bureaucracy in Action (page 249)
Answer: #2

8. The World of Fashion (page 269)
Answer: #1

9. Stupidity at Work (page 284)
Answer: #2

10. The Rocky Road to Love (page 297)
Answer: #2

THE LAST PAGE

All good things must come to an end and now is the time to stand up and be counted.

We thank you for your support, and, as always, we look forward to your thoughts, comments, critiques, and (we hope) approval.

For correspondence or comments, contact us at:
Uncle John's Presents
Portable Press
5880 Oberlin Drive
San Diego, CA 92121

E-mail: unclejohn@advmkt.com

And please consider this your gold-plated invitation to become a member of the Bathroom Reader Society. To join, please contact us through our members' Web site (www.bathroomreader.com).

Look for new Uncle John's Presents productions, coming soon to bookstores everywhere:

Uncle John's Presents: The Great State of Texas
Uncle John's Presents: The Book of Moms
Uncle John's Bathroom Reader Puzzle Book #2
Uncle John's Bathroom Reader for Kids Only #3

Enjoy!